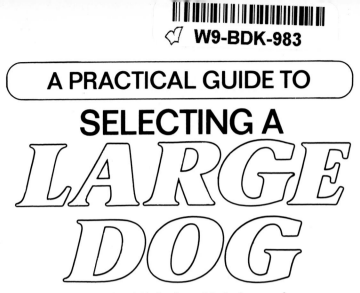

A PRACTICAL GUIDE TO

SELECTING A
LARGE DOG

**An Illustrated guide designed to help you choose
the most suitable large dog for you and your
home from over 80 international breeds**

JOAN PALMER

St Bernard

No. 16019

A Salamander Book

© 1987 Salamander Books Ltd.,
129 - 137 York Way
London N79LG
United Kingdom

ISBN 1-56465-135-5

Library of Congress No. 87-050362

All correspondence concerning the
content of this volume should be
addressed to Tetra Press.

Publishers note: Some material in this
book has previously appeared in *A Dog
of Your Own* and *An Illustrated Guide to
Dogs.*

Credits

Editors: Geoff Rogers, Charlotte
Mortensson
Designers: Roger Hyde, Paul Johnson
Colour artwork: John Francis (Linden
Artists), John Green (John Martin &
Artists) © Salamander Books Ltd.
Line drawings: Glenn Steward (John
Martin & Artists) © Salamander
Books Ltd.
Filmset: Modern Text Typesetting Ltd.,
England
Colour reproductions: Bantam Litho
Ltd., England

Printed in Belgium

Picture Credits

The publishers wish to thank the following photographers and agencies who have
supplied photographs for this book.

Animal Photography Ltd.
3, 6, 10, 13, 14, 18, 20, 21, 22, 23, 24,
25, 26, 27, 28, 29, 43, 45, 46, 48, 49,
53, 78, 79, 80, 81, 82, 84, 86, 87, 88,
90, 91, 92, 95, 97, 98, 99, 102, 103,
105, 108, 111, 112, 113, 114, 117

Marc Henrie
Front cover, back cover,
7, 8, 9, 11, 12, 34, 38, 40, 44, 51,
56, 75, 76, 83, 93, 94, 96, 104, 107,
115, 116

Gloria Hoskins
100

Robert Pearcy
30

Syndication International
17, 47, 54

Contents

Text and colour illustrations are cross-referenced throughout as follows: 52▸
The breeds are arranged in order of increasing weight. Page numbers in roman type refer to text entries; those in **bold** to colour illustrations.

Introduction

Large dogs make wonderful companions. Their physical make-up enables them to accompany their owners on lengthy treks and their sheer presence is reassuring.

It would be a mistake, however, to think that a large dog will fit happily into any environment and lifestyle. A study of the breed profiles in this book will reveal that many large dogs have been bred for a specific purpose such as hunting, herding or guarding and may prove to be totally unsuitable for the type of life and the facilities you are able to offer it.

As a general guide, terriers are lively dogs which make good pets, but as they were bred to hunt small mammals such as rats and foxes, they are often snappy. Gundogs (known as bird dogs in the USA) are usually gentle, affectionate animals which adapt well to the dual role of sportsman's dog and children's pet. Hounds have a tendency to wander off and are not renowned for their obedience. Working breeds—the category into which most of the shepherd and guarding breeds fall—are best suited to an environment in which they can perform a function as close as possible to that for which they have been bred for many generations.

It would, therefore, be a mistake to buy a gentle Retriever and expect it to be a fierce guard dog, or to buy a guard dog such as a German Shepherd Dog, a Dobermann or a Rottweiler, unless you have the patience and the time to devote to its training. When choosing your dog you must also bear in mind how much grooming it will need. Long-coated breeds such as the Afghan

Above: Gundogs, such as the Large Munsterlander, make gentle loyal pets.

Above: The Mastiff, a natural guard dog, is happiest if kept in the country.

Hound require much more time spent on their coats than, for example, the sleek-coated Weimaraner or the Labrador Retriever. People who are especially houseproud should also remember that some dogs, such as the Dalmatian, shed their coats all year round.

Buying Your Large Dog

Once you have decided on the type of dog you want to buy you should contact your national kennel club and ask for names and addresses of breeders of that variety. You may also like to query dates and venues of dog shows to be held in your area. It is a good idea to visit one or two shows so that you can examine the breeds which interest you at close quarters and ask the breeders any questions that you may have. You can also find out whether they are likely to have a litter of puppies available in the near future.

Dog or Bitch?

You will need to decide whether you want to buy a dog or a bitch. The bitch usually has a gentler nature than the dog. She is almost always chosen for obedience work and makes a reliable pet. The dog has a more rumbustious nature and is constantly attracted to the opposite sex, unlike the bitch which does not look for a male companion except during her twice-yearly season. However, some people prefer the dog's more zestful and enthusiastic approach to life.

Pet or Show Dog?

It is a common mistake to think that because a dog has a certificate of pedigree it can be termed a show dog and that it is likely to win prizes. A certificate of pedigree only proves that the dog is the progeny of a sire and dam of the same breed with a bloodline that can be traced back for some generations. Each pure bred type of dog has what is known as a Breed Standard laid down by its national kennel club. The Standard clearly states those characteristics and physical attributes which add up to a perfect specimen of the breed, for instance, the desired temperament, coat colour and texture, height, weight and other points. The dog which conforms most exactly, in both temperament and appearance, with its Breed Standard will be picked out by an experienced judge in the show ring.

Most pure bred dogs are not show dogs. This does not mean that they are not good examples of their breed but simply that they may be a fraction too large or too small, have a tail which is set too high or too low or are mis-marked. Such variations from the Standard will bar the dog from successfully competing against its fellows.

If you want a show dog the breeder will pick out a promising show prospect for you, but bear in mind that a puppy's development cannot be forecast with any degree of certainty until it is six months old.

Documents

When you go to collect your puppy the breeder should give you a certificate of pedigree and also a form enabling you to transfer its ownership into your name with your national kennel club. It is important that you receive these documents and effect the transfer. If you fail to do this you will run into problems if you want to enter the puppy in shows or if you want to breed from your bitch or offer your dog for stud purposes.

You should ask the breeder about the puppy's worming programme and whether it has had its vaccinations. If it has had its jabs you will need the veterinary record card so that you can check when booster inoculations fall due.

A reputable breeder will not object to the purchase being made subject to a veterinary examination. If the dog is found to be unfit it should be—and is by law in the United Kingdom—returnable to the source of purchase for a full refund of the money paid. However, a veterinary certificate stating the reason for return must be produced. Adult dogs should be bought with a seven or fourteen day warranty whereby they can be returned to the seller if found unsuitable because of vice or other genuine reason. Most breeders are only too happy to provide such a service as they value the good name of their kennels.

Above: The Airedale, the largest of the terrier breeds, will adapt to town life.

Above: These boxer pups have yet to be weaned.

Feeding

Before taking your puppy home you should ensure that it is
properly weaned. You can ask the breeder if you may see the
puppy eat a little food. Breeders generally encourage a litter to
begin taking some solid food from about three weeks of age,
but it is unlikely that they will be completely weaned onto it
before they are six or seven weeks old. It is inadvisable to buy
a puppy under eight weeks of age.

When buying a puppy you should ask the breeder for a diet
sheet and strictly adhere to it for the first fortnight before
introducing any gradual changes.

Puppies should be given four meals a day until they are
three months of age—breakfast, lunch, tea and supper, because
at this stage they cannot digest their total food ration in one
serving. Breakfast and supper may consist of a dry, branded
baby food mixed with milk and a little sugar and the evening
meal could be an egg swished in milk. However, lunch and tea
should be primarily meat meals, for example lightly cooked,
lean minced beef supplemented by puppy meal or biscuit in the
proportion of three parts meat to two parts biscuit. Some
owners prefer to rear their large dogs on raw meat, particularly
guard dogs. This is a matter of personal preference.

When a puppy reaches four months of age the evening feed
can be omitted and at six months breakfast can be stopped.
By the time the dog is one year old—when it is deemed to be an
adult—it should be receiving only one meal a day.

Above: Labrador Retrievers have a tendency to put on weight if not sufficiently exercised.

There are some large breeds which make particularly rapid growth during the first months of life and need to be fed constantly. Others, like the Estrela Mountain Dog, prefer a light diet, green tripe being a favourite dish. If you are in any doubt as to your puppy's progress you should consult your veterinarian.

You will note from each of the breed profiles the expected weight and, in some cases, the height of an adult dog. However, there are dogs kept as pets, for instance Labrador Retrievers and Dalmatians, which are larger or smaller than their Breed Standards dictate. They therefore require slightly larger or smaller rations than those laid down for a dog of their expected size. Also, it must be remembered that the working dog uses more energy than the pet dog and therefore needs more food.

Puppies have the same basic nutritional requirements as adult dogs but their food must be easily digestible, and contain a large quantity of body building protein as well as minerals and vitamins to maintain the puppy's quick rate of growth.

New puppies can sometimes prove to be finicky eaters. This problem can usually be overcome by a variety of methods ranging from pretending to offer the dish to another pet (when there is one) to adding an appetizer such as a vegetable extract to the meal. It is unwise to resort to drastic measures such as feeding only chicken pieces or you could find yourself with a pet which will turn up its nose at normal canine fare thereafter.

Do not feed your dog scraps from the table. This habit will only result in a pet with a thickened waistline. It will also become a nuisance, constantly pawing and cadging for titbits whenever there is food around. However, do make sure that it receives its meal at the same time every day. Dogs are creatures of habit and look forward to their mealtime as much as we look forward to our own. It does not matter whether you give the adult dog its feed at midday or in the early evening as long as the time is consistent.

Exercise and Good Health

Before you take your dog for its first walk outside it must be vaccinated against the main killer diseases—distemper, infectious hepatitis, two forms of leptospirosis and canine parvovirus—it will also need booster inoculations at regular intervals thereafter which your veterinarian will advise you about.

Highly effective vaccines, free from side effects, are now available to combat these diseases and are usually administered at about ten weeks of age consisting of two injections with a two to three week interval between them. There is also a vaccine against rabies which is recommended for dogs living in countries where this scourge is endemic. In some places such as the United States rabies vaccinations are required by law. They are unnecessary in rabies-free zones such as Australasia and the United Kingdom.

It is also necessary for your pup to be wormed. Puppies should be wormed at intervals of one to two weeks from three weeks of age up to six months and thereafter at six monthly intervals. However the recommended treatment can vary in different parts of the world and it is as well to seek a veterinarian's advice. Special attention should also be given to worming the bitch in whelp.

Once your pup has had its vaccinations you can enjoy taking it out for exercise. However, it is inadvisable to subject it to really long, strenuous walks until it is six months of age. Once it has reached six months it is sensible to take the pup to a dog training class where you will be taught how to control it properly and to learn the basics of obedience training.

Just as the dog looks forward to its regular mealtime so it looks forward to regular exercise periods and the dog that has become accustomed to its early morning and evening walk will be found at the appropriate time waiting by the door or adopting other obvious tactics to remind its owner that it is ready to be taken out.

Above: All dogs should have their own chair, blanket or basket to rest on.

Above: An outdoor kennel should be clean, dry and draught-free.

As a rule, a good twenty or thirty minutes walk twice a day, should be sufficient for a large dog, especially if the owner lives near an open space where it can safely be allowed off the leash. If there are occasions when you cannot fulfil this obligation the dog can be exercised by retrieving a ball or some other object in the garden, but games should not become a substitute for daily walks. The large, energetic dog that is shut up for many hours and given insufficient exercise is likely to become a bored and even destructive one.

Most large breeds adapt well to car travel and it is a good idea to invest in a dog guard, which partitions off the rear of the vehicle, preventing the dog from clambering into the driving area. Never leave a dog in a car without making sure that there is a window open allowing sufficient ventilation. This advice refers to all breeds, particularly flat-nosed ones.

If you wish to exhibit your large dog you may decide to buy an indoor kennel which can also be used as a carrier crate and will fold flat in the boot of your car. Such kennels, which are made in a wide range of sizes, are constructed of sturdy wire mesh. They are easy to erect and have a removable base tray. They are, therefore, ideal for the owner who wishes to safely leave a pup for a few hours during the toilet training and teething stage. The pup's basket can be put in the kennel, together with its water bowl, and the kennel base lined with newspaper. It is rare for a puppy, far less an adult dog, to soil its bed and newspaper is easily discarded.

Whether a large dog is to live indoors as a member of the family or be kennelled outside must be a matter of choice. Owners with several large dogs may find it impractical for them all to live indoors and some people are of the opinion that it is softening for a working dog. Certainly large, thick-coated breeds will come to no harm in outdoor quarters provided that they have a specially constructed kennel which enables them to stand, turn about and curl up in comfort. They must have adequate bedding and be protected from extremes of temperature. It is possible to buy a kennel with an adjoining exercise run and it is obviously beneficial if this additional facility can be provided.

If the decision is made to kennel your large dog outside it is essential that it should not be forgotten for hours on end. It must be visited frequently to ensure that it is has adequate fresh water, that its kennel is clean and that it is fed, groomed and regularly let out for proper exercise.

In conclusion, please do not even think of buying a large dog if your aim is to keep it just as a burglar alarm, constantly chained up. All dogs need affection and a liberal amount of freedom. To chain a dog continually is not only cruel, but in some places it is also illegal.

Fortunately, most people who buy a large dog want it to be their companion and share their life. This is the role to which it is best suited and it will reward its owner a hundred-fold with devotion, loyalty and companionship.

Above: The supremely intelligent German Shepherd Dog is a natural guard dog, which also makes a first-class companion.

SHAR-PEI (Chinese Fighting Dog)

Good points
- *Excellent watchdog*
- *Loyal to owner*
- *Amiable unless provoked*
- *Highly intelligent*
- *Good with children*

Take heed
- *May be more susceptible to disease than other imports, which have built up immunity*

The Shar-Pei has recently lost the distinction of being listed in the *Guinness Book of Records* as the rarest dog in the world and interest in this breed is increasing particularly in the United Kingdom and USA.

What does it look like? Descriptions vary from a dog that looks as if its skin is several sizes too big for it, to a Bloodhound, but with wrinkles all over.

The Shar-Pei has small, rectangular ears that point towards the eyes, a tail that forms a circle, its tip touching its base, and stiff short hair that stands up. It is likely that its rarity will be short-lived, for at a recent reckoning many Shar-Peis were in the kennels of Mr Ernest Albright of California,

the man largely responsible for saving the Shar-Pei from extinction. There are also now a handful of Shar-Peis scattered throughout the United States and Canada, the owners of which will doubtless perpetuate the breed, the future of which was put in peril when, in 1947, the tax on dogs in the People's Republic of China rose so steeply that few people could afford to keep them and many were utilized as food.

There are now also Shar-Peis in the UK, where their population is steadily rising.

It is an extremely intelligent dog,

Below: The Shar-Pei is an intelligent dog which fits well into family life.

an excellent guard, and amiable unless provoked, and it enjoys human companionship; it is also most affectionate, an added advantage being that Shar-Pei pups are said to house-train themselves!

Size
Weight: 18.1-22.7kg (40-50lb).
Height: 46-51cm (18-20in) at the withers.

Exercise
The Shar-Pei — or, to give it its former name, the Chinese Fighting Dog — was used to hunt wild boar and to herd flocks. It is a breed more suited to those with large gardens, or living near areas where it may unleash its energies, and it needs good daily walks and off-the-lead runs.

It will interest obedience enthusiasts to learn that 'Chin', a Shar-Pei trained by Ernest Albright in the United States, has won three ribbons in obedience trials.

Feeding
In their land of origin these dogs are undoubtedly fed on rice, a diet that has resulted in instances of rickets and other ailments associated with malnutrition. The Shar-Pei is a hardy dog and, if fed correctly, should have few health problems. The branded canned food requirement for a dog of its size is approximately 1½ cans (376g, 13.3oz size) per day, with the usual biscuit supplement.

Health care
The breed is susceptible to entropion, an eye disease that can cause blindness if the lashes penetrate the cornea. The disease is curable, and a veterinarian should be consulted at any sign of eye irritation.

A unique feature of this breed is that heat in the female can be at irregular intervals, and with some females the season may not occur until she is 15 months of age or more. Also, when the Shar-Pei is in season, she will not attract the attention of males of other breeds, and only of certain members of her own breed, so planned mating calls for vigilant surveillance.

Origin and history
Works of art depicting a likeness to the Shar-Pei survive from the Han Dynasty (206 BC to AD 220).

It is possible that the Shar-Pei originated in Tibet or the Northern Province of China about 20 centuries ago, when it was probably a much larger dog than it is now, weighing 38.6-74.8kg (85-165lb). Other sources maintain that the Shar-Pei is a descendant of the Service Dogs that, for thousands of years, lived in the Southern Province near the South China Sea.

Certainly, for hundreds of years it lived up to its name of Chinese Fighting Dog; it was provoked, and then matched against other dogs for the owner's profit, the loose skin of the Shar-Pei making it difficult for its opponent to get a firm grip on its body. It is said that drugs were used to heighten the breed's aggression, for it is basically a loving and gentle animal. 57▶

BULLDOG

Good points
- *Courageous and intelligent*
- *Good tempered*
- *Loves children*

Take heed
- *Best suited to a temperate climate — excessive heat causes heart attacks*
- *Snores*
- *Not built for strenuous exercise*

The Bulldog, despite its somewhat ferocious appearance, has a docile temperament and generally adores children. It is quick to learn and will enjoy taking part in games. However, its build precludes any fast running, and it must never be allowed to rush about in hot weather, as its nose does not equip it for rapid breathing. It should never be shut in a car or other confined space unless plenty of fresh air is available.

This breed is not renowned for longevity. It can, however, be warmly recommended as a loyal guard and lovable family pet.

Size
Dog: 25kg (55lb). Bitch: 22.7kg (50lb).

Exercise
The Bulldog will benefit from a good daily walk on a loose lead. If the owner lives in a safe, rural area, or has a nearby enclosed park, the dog will enjoy being allowed off the lead so that it may amble at its own pace. But please don't drag it, or let it over-exert itself as a pup. Experience will show how much exercise it enjoys without tiring.

Grooming
A daily brushing with a fairly stiff brush and a rub-down with a hound glove will keep the Bulldog in good condition. Choose a warm summer's day for its annual bath!

Feeding
The Bulldog needs a full can (376g, 13.3oz) of branded dog food or 454g (1lb) of raw meat daily, with the addition of biscuit meal. A daily teaspoonful of cod liver oil is recommended in winter as a body builder. It is best to feed after exercise so that the meal may digest while the dog sleeps.

Origin and history
This breed can be traced back to the Molossus, the fighting dog of the ancient Greek tribe at Athens called the Molossi. However, the Mastiff would seem to resemble this powerful breed more faithfully, which suggests that the Mastiff, Bulldog and Boxer may have a common ancestor. Certainly they were all fighting dogs: the Mastiff fought against both gladiators and wild beasts in the arenas of Rome, and the Boxer was known in Germany as 'Bullenbeisser' or bull-baiter.

It is, however, the Bulldog that is generally associated with the unpleasant 'sport' of bull-baiting — seizing the bull by the nose and holding it until it fell. The sport was promoted by a certain Earl Warren of Stamford, Lincolnshire, who, after enjoying the spectacle of two dogs fighting bulls in 1209, sought to bring such a sight to a wider audience.

When bull-baiting became illegal in 1838, the Bulldog was in danger of extinction, for it appeared to have served its purpose. However, a Mr Bill George continued to breed Bulldogs, and to him a debt of gratitude is due in that the breed, despite its fearsome countenance, has developed into a much esteemed, reliable pet.

57▶

SIBERIAN HUSKY

Good points
- *Healthy*
- *Adaptable*
- *Friendly*
- *Good with children*
- *Intelligent*
- *Reliable*
- *Good guard dog*

Take heed
- *Needs lots of exercise*

The Siberian Husky is perhaps the most friendly of all Arctic Spitz breeds, having a long history of friendship with man, combining the roles of household companion with work-mate, hauling the sled or herding. It is faithful and reliable.

Size
Height at the withers: dog 53-60cm (21-23½in); bitch 51-56cm (20-22in). Weight: dog 20.5-27.2kg (45-60lb); bitch 15.9-22.7kg (35-50lb). Weight should be in proportion to height.

Exercise
Famed for sled racing, remarkable endurance and great powers of speed, this is not a dog to keep confined in a small back yard.

Grooming
Regular brushing will keep the coat in good condition.

Feeding
Recommended would be 1½-2½ cans (376g, 13.3oz size) of a branded meaty product, with biscuit added in equal part by volume; or 5 cupfuls of a dry food, complete diet, mixed in the proportion of 1 cup of feed to ½ cup of hot or cold water.

Origin and history
The Siberian Husky was bred by the nomadic Chukchi tribes of north-east Asia. Their purpose in breeding the Husky, from other local dogs, was to produce a hardy animal of great endurance, that would combine the roles of companion and hunter with that of a speedy sled dog which, at times, would be their only means of transport.

More recently, the Siberian Husky has been recognized as a show dog. It performed creditably as a Search and Rescue dog for the American Air Force in World War II, and has popularized the sport of sled racing in America and elsewhere in the world. 58▶

Below: The Siberian Husky, a legend for its speed and endurance.

SAMOYED

Good points
- *Beautiful appearance*
- *Devoted to owner*
- *Obedient*
- *Intelligent*
- *Very hardy*
- *Good show dog*

Take heed
- *Slightly independent*
- *That white coat sheds*

The Samoyed, or 'Sammy' as it is often called, is a beautiful, somewhat independent breed that should, according to its standard, show 'marked affection for all mankind'. These dogs adore the snow and are happiest in the wide open spaces. But having said that, I know of some living happily in semi-detached houses, and one that has become a TV star.

Size
Height at the shoulder: dog 51-56cm (20-22in); bitch 46-51cm (18-20in). Weight should be in proportion to size.

Below: The handsome Samoyed, a strong and faithful working dog.

Exercise
Needs a liberal amount of exercise and, if possible, some obedience work, even if this is only weekly attendance at a dog training club — which, after all, is recommended for all breeds.

Grooming
Regular brushing and combing, and a towelling after getting wet. The under-coat sheds once a year: at such times it is best to comb out as much surplus hair as one can. Bathing helps, as this tends to loosen the hair.

Feeding
Recommended would be 1½-2½ cans (376g, 13.3oz size) of a branded meaty product, with biscuit added in equal part by volume; or 5 cupfuls of a dry food, complete diet, mixed in the proportion of 1 cup of feed to ½ cup of hot or cold water.

Origin and history
The Samoyed is a beautiful Spitz-type that takes its name from the Siberian tribe of the Samoyedes. It is a sled dog in its native country, and is also used as a guard and herder of reindeer. Some Sammies were used by the explorer Nansen on his journey to the North Pole.

The breed came to Britain in 1889, and much of the present-day stock can be traced to the original pair. British stock has done much to popularize the breed in other countries of the world. 58▶

STANDARD POODLE

Good points
- *Good temperament*
- *Intelligent*
- *Splendid retriever*
- *Usually good with children and other dogs*

Take heed
- *Do not make a clown or fashion model out of a fundamentally outdoor type*

The Poodle has a character full of fun. It is intelligent and obedient. In the United Kingdom it has proved a useful competitor in obedience competitions. It has a fondness for water, if the owner permits, but is much favoured for the show ring where, exhibited in the traditional lion clip, it is a beauty to behold. It is also, debatably, the most difficult breed to prepare for the ring, involving the handler in a day's canine beauty treatment.

The Breed Standard states: 'A very active, intelligent, well-balanced and elegant-looking dog with good temperament, carrying itself very proudly.'

Size
Height: 38cm (15in) and over. Present day Standard Poodles may be seen measuring 63.5cm (25in) or more at the shoulder.

Exercise
This is a robust, healthy dog that loves the outdoors, has plenty of stamina and has lost none of its retrieving sporting instincts. It will enjoy plenty of exercise.

Grooming
Use a wire-pin pneumatic brush and a wire-toothed metal comb for daily grooming. The lion clip is an essential for the show ring, but pet owners generally resort to the more natural lamb clip with the hair a short uniform length. It is possible to clip your own dog with a pair of hairdressers' scissors. However, if, despite the help which is usually available from the breeder, you find the task tedious, there are numerous pet and poodle parlours to which you should take your dog every six weeks. Bath regularly.

Feeding
About 1½ cans (376g, 13.3oz size) of a branded, meaty product, with biscuit added in equal part by volume; or 3 cupfuls of a dry, complete food, mixed in the proportion of 1 cup of feed to ½ cup of hot or cold water.

If you are using your Poodle as a working dog then these amounts may need to be increased.

Origin and history
The Poodle was originally a shaggy guard, a retriever and protector of sheep, with origins similar to the Irish Water Spaniel and, no doubt, a common ancestor in the French Barbet and Hungarian Water Hound.

The Poodle may not be, as many suppose, solely of French origin. It originated in Germany as a water retriever; even the word poodle comes from the German 'pudelnass' or puddle. From this fairly large sturdy dog, the Standard Poodle, the Miniature and the Toy have evolved.

The breed has been known in England since Prince Rupert of the Rhine, in company with his Poodle, came to the aid of Charles I in battle. The breed was favoured also by Marie Antoinette who, rumour has it, invented the lion clip by devising a style which would match the uniform of her courtiers. It is also popular in the United States. 58▶

19

ENGLISH SPRINGER SPANIEL

Good points
- *Excellent with children*
- *Good worker in the field*
- *Intelligent*
- *Loyal*
- *Good house pet*

Take heed
- *Could develop skin trouble and/or put on weight, if under-exercised*

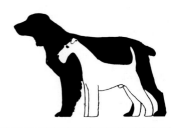

The English Springer Spaniel makes an excellent dual-purpose gundog and pet. It gives a good account of itself in obedience competitions and excels as a happy, efficient retriever.

Size
The approximate height should be 51cm (20in). The approximate weight should be 22.7kg (50lb).

Exercise
Needs plenty of exercise, or is likely to put on weight. Lack of exercise often leads to skin troubles, too.

Grooming
Daily brushing. Take care that mud does not become caked in the paws, and make sure that the ears are kept clean and tangle-free to prevent infection.

Feeding
One to 1½ cans (376g, 13.3oz size) of a branded meaty product, with biscuit added in equal part by volume; or 3 cupfuls of a dry food, complete diet, mixed in the proportion of 1 cup of feed to ½ cup of hot or cold water.

Origin and history
The English Springer is the oldest of the British spaniels except for the Clumber, but it has never gained the popularity of the smaller Cocker Spaniel, tending to be favoured, in the main, by those with an interest in shooting and/or field trials. Incidentally, the English Springer was appreciated by the Americans as a 'bird'

Above: The English Springer Spaniel needs regular grooming and plenty of long energetic walks.

dog before it had even been recognized by the Kennel Club in London. Certainly the name 'springer' is derived from its early task of 'springing' game for the hunter's nets. The slightly smaller Sussex Spaniel, known in Southern England for more than a century, has a rich liver-coloured coat which darkens if the dog is kept indoors. Sadly, it is in danger of extinction.

59▶

IRISH WATER SPANIEL

Good points
- *Brave*
- *Easily trained*
- *Excellent retriever*
- *Strong swimmer*
- *Equable temperament*
- *Intelligent*
- *Loving*

Take heed
- *No drawbacks known*

The Irish Water Spaniel is a most attractive animal, loyal, intelligent and with a deeply affectionate nature. It is an excellent retriever and a strong, fearless swimmer, most useful for wildfowling.

Size
Height: dog 53-58.5cm (21-23in); bitch 51-56cm (20-22in).

Exercise
Needs plenty of exercise.

Grooming
Daily brushing and weekly combing. Seek advice on stripping of unwanted hair. Take care that mud does not become caked in the toes.

Feeding
One to 1½ cans (376g, 13.3oz size) of a branded meaty product, with biscuit added in equal part by volume; or 3 cupfuls of a dry food, complete diet, mixed in the proportion of 1 cup of feed to ½ cup of hot or cold water.

Origin and history
This dog was developed in Ireland from several spaniel breeds towards the end of the 19th century. Unfortunately, perhaps, it has never gained immense popularity. The American Water Spaniel is thought to have derived from crossing the Irish Water Spaniel with a smaller spaniel breed and/or with a Curly-coated Retriever. 58▶

Below: As happy in the water as on the land, the strong and intelligent Irish Water Spaniel excels in retrieving wildfowl.

ELKHOUND (Norwegian Elkhound)

Good points
- *Intelligent and alert*
- *Good household pet*
- *Lacks doggy odour*
- *Reliable with children*
- *Sensible guard*

Take heed
- *Needs firm but gentle discipline in puppyhood*
- *Thrives on vigorous exercise*

The Elkhound is a happy breed, loyal and devoted to its master and reliable with children. It has a great love of the outdoors, is energetic, and is not recommended for those unable to provide exercise.

Size
Height at shoulder: dog 52cm (20½in); bitch 49.5cm (19½in). Weight: dog 22.7kg (50lb); bitch 19.5kg (43lb).

Exercise
Needs plenty of exercise in open spaces to stay healthy.

Grooming
Daily brushing and combing.

Feeding
One to 1½ cans (376g, 13.3oz size) of a branded meaty product, with biscuit added in equal part by volume; or 3 cupfuls of a dry food,

complete diet, mixed in the proportion of 1 cup of feed to ½ cup of hot or cold water.

Origin and history
The job of the Elkhound was to seek out the elk and hold it at bay until its master moved in for the kill. It has existed in Norway for centuries, but was not considered a show prospect until 1877 when the Norwegian Hunter's Association first held a show.

Today's Elkhound has been tailored to meet the ideal decided upon by various Scandinavian clubs and societies, and has become its national breed. There is a miniature variety rarely seen outside Scandinavia, from which the puffin hunting Lundehund was derived. 57▶

Below: The Elkhound, a hardy and lively breed from Scandinavia.

SWEDISH ELKHOUND (Jämthund)

Good points
- Brave
- Intelligent
- Equable temperament
- Excellent hunter
- Good guard dog

Take heed
- No drawbacks known, but remember it is essentially a hunter

The Swedish Elkhound is little known outside its native country, where its popularity surpasses that of the Norwegian Elkhound. It has great stamina and makes a bold and energetic hunter. It is also an excellent guard. It is loyal to its master, of a calm temperament, and extremely agile.

Size
Dog 58.5-63.5cm (23-25in), bitch 53-58.5cm (21-23in).

Exercise
Needs plenty of exercise.

Grooming
Daily brushing and combing.

Below: The Swedish Elkhound, the largest of the Elkhound types.

Feeding
One to 1½ cans (376g, 13.3oz size) of a branded meaty product, with biscuit added in equal part by volume; or 3 cupfuls of a dry food, complete diet, mixed in the proportion of 1 cup of feed to ½ cup of hot or cold water.

Origin and history
The Swedish Elkhound is similar to the Norwegian Elkhound, but despite continuing popularity in its country of origin it is little known elsewhere— unlike the Norwegian Elkhound, which has had universal success in the show ring.

The breed was evolved by Swedish huntsmen who considered their local Spitz breeds superior to the Norwegian Elkhound for hunting. 59▶

KARELIAN BEAR DOG

Good points
- *Striking appearance*
- *Brave*
- *Fine hunter*
- *Hardy*
- *Loyal to its owner*

Take heed
- *Does not get on with other dogs*
- *Unsuitable as a family pet*

The Karelian Bear Dog is a sturdy hunter of bear and elk. It is a brave dog, and loyal to its master. It does not get on with other dogs and can not, ideally, be recommended as a family pet.

Size
Height at shoulder: 53-61cm (21-24in) for dogs, 48-53cm (19-21in) for bitches.

Exercise
Needs plenty of exercise in open spaces to stay healthy.

Grooming
Daily brushing will keep the coat in good condition.

Feeding
One to 1½ cans (376g, 13.3oz size) of a branded meaty product, with biscuit added in equal part by volume; or 3 cupfuls of a dry food, complete diet, mixed in the proportion of 1 cup of feed to ½ cup of hot or cold water.

Origin and history
The Karelian Bear Dog is a Spitz belonging to the Russian breed of Laikas, but this type evolved in Finland. It is known throughout Scandinavia as a fearless hunter of bear and elk. (The Russians decreed, in 1947, that only four distinct types of Spitz should in future be referred to as Laikas, and these are neither known nor exported outside the USSR.) 59▶

Below: The tenacious Karelian Bear Dog – hardy but fierce.

BEAUCERON
(Beauce Shepherd, Bas-rouge, French Short-haired Shepherd, Berger de la Beauce)

Good points
- *Brave*
- *Faithful*
- *Easily trained*
- *Fine guard*
- *Intelligent*

Take heed
- *Ferocious if roused*
- *Needs a job to do*

The Beauceron is a guard and herder of supreme intelligence and loyalty. It resembles the Dobermann in appearance.

Size
Height at shoulder: dog 63.5-71cm (25-28in); bitch 61-68.5cm (24-27in).

Exercise
Happiest when working or exercising in the wide open spaces.

Grooming
Regular brushing will keep the coat in good condition.

Feeding
Recommended would be 1½-2½ cans (376g, 13.3oz size) of a branded meaty product, with biscuit added in equal part by volume; or 5 cupfuls of a dry food,

Above: The powerful Beauceron makes an effective guard dog.

complete diet, mixed in the proportion of 1 cup of feed to ½ cup of hot or cold water.

Origin and history
The Beauceron belongs to the four best-known herding breeds of France, all of which derive from different areas, the others being the Briard, Picardy and Pyrenean Mountain Dog. The Beauceron resembles the Dobermann in both colour and appearance. It has come down from an old, less refined shepherd dog, probably used also for hunting, and has been established in its present form only since the end of last century. It is a natural herder, and in recent years its temperament has been greatly improved. 59▶

CLUMBER SPANIEL

Good points
- *Striking appearance*
- *Even temperament*
- *Intelligent*
- *Reliable*
- *Excellent nose*
- *Easy to train*

Take heed
- *Slow but sure worker*
- *Prefers the outdoor life*

The Clumber is the heaviest of the spaniels and is thought to be of French origin, brought about by crossing the Basset Hound with the Alpine Spaniel (which is now extinct).

It is a brave, attractive and reliable dog; a slow but sure worker that excels for rough shooting and is an excellent retriever.

Size
Dog about 25-32kg (55-70lb); bitch about 20.5-27kg (45-60lb).

Exercise
This is essentially a working dog, best suited to country life and needs plenty of exercise and off-the-lead runs in open spaces.

Grooming
Routine brushing. Keep coat tangle free and take care that mud does not become lodged between the toes.

Feeding
Recommended would be 1½-2½ cans of a branded meaty product (376g, 13.3oz size), with biscuit added in equal part by volume; or 5 cupfuls of a dry food, complete diet, mixed in the proportion of 1 cup of feed to ½ cup of hot or cold water. Rations should be stepped up or decreased, according to the amount of work the dog is asked to do.

Origin and history
The Clumber Spaniel was fostered and promoted by the Duc de Noailles in the years before the

Above: Clumber Spaniels are massively built dogs with a thoughtful expression and a characteristic rolling gait. They make slow but reliable working dogs as beaters and retrievers.

French Revolution. The breed became renowned as beaters and retrievers in the field.

With the advent of war, the Duc de Noailles brought his dogs to England and entrusted them to the Duke of Newcastle at Clumber Park, from which the name is derived. The Duc de Noailles was killed in the revolution, but fortunately he left the legacy of his spaniels in England. 59▶

HARRIER

Good points
- *Strongly built*
- *First-rate hunter*
- *Lively*
- *Hardy*

Take heed
- *Noisy*
- *This breed does not make a suitable pet*

The Harrier bears some similarity to the Beagle but more closely resembles the Foxhound, with which it has been so interbred that few purebred Harriers exist today. It is slower than the Beagle and Foxhound and is generally used to hunt the hare on both foot and horseback, although it is also used for foxhunting.

Size
Height varies from 46 to 56cm (18-22in).

Exercise
Needs liberal amounts of exercise.

Grooming
Use a hound glove.

Below: Like the Foxhounds, which it resembles, the Harrier is not really suitable as a family pet. It is essentially a hunting breed.

Feeding
As for Foxhounds (see page 153)

Origin and history
The Harrier is extremely popular in the United States but is, in fact, an ancient British breed, the first pack of which was recorded in the year 1260. This pack, the Penistone, was established by Sir Elias de Midhope and existed for over five centuries. The word 'harrier' is Norman French for 'hunting dog', and at one time all hunting dogs in Britain were known as Harriers. The breed is similar in appearance to the Foxhound. Primarily used for fox and rabbit hunting, it has an additional, unexpected chore in South America and Ceylon, where it is used for leopard hunting. Harriers are exhibited in dog shows in the United States. It is also popular with the American drag hunt. 60 ▶

HAMILTON HOUND (Hamiltonstövare)

Good points
- *First-rate scent hound*
- *Lively*
- *Affectionate*
- *Intelligent*
- *Good companion dog*

Take heed
- *Has a loud resonant bay in common with other hunting dogs*
- *Needs lots of exercise*

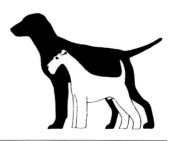

The Hamilton is not a pack dog, but is kept singly or in pairs in the homes of its owners. It is used to flush game for the guns in Sweden's large coniferous forests. It is intelligent, trainable, and a good companion and house dog. This medium-sized hound was named after Count Hamilton, who created the breed by crossing the English Foxhound with the best German hounds, including the Holstein Hound and the Hanoverian Haidbracke. It is the most popular hunting hound in Sweden. Count Hamilton was the founder of the Swedish Kennel Club.

Below: The Hamilton Hound, an elegant hunter from Sweden.

Size
Height at the shoulder: dog 49.5-58.5cm (19½-23in): bitch 46-57cm (18-22½in).

Exercise
Requires plenty of strenuous exercise to stay in good condition.

Grooming
Use a hound glove.

Feeding
One to 1½ cans (376g, 13.3oz size) of a branded meaty product, with biscuit added in equal part by volume; or 3 cupfuls of a dry food, complete diet, mixed in the proportion of 1 cup of feed to ½ cup of hot or cold water.

ENGLISH FOXHOUND

Good points
- *Strongly built*
- *First-rate hunter*
- *Lively*
- *Full of stamina*

Take heed
- *Noisy*
- *This breed does not make a suitable pet*

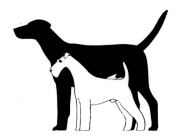

The Foxhound is not suitable as a household pet. It is almost always the property of a foxhunting pack. Hunt supporters often take on the role of puppy walker, in order to accustom a young hound to road hazards and livestock before returning it to its pack. Hounds are attractive, vivacious pups, but far too active and destructive for the average household. It is not possible in the United Kingdom to purchase a Foxhound as a pet. Hounds are always counted by the pack in couples: the huntsman will talk of having 30 couples.

Size
Height: dog 58.5cm (23in); bitch just a little less.

Exercise
Vigorous exercise is necessary. Foxhounds should have the stamina to spend all day running foxes with the hunt.

Below: A pack of English Foxhounds waiting for the hunt to begin.

Grooming
Use a hound glove.

Feeding
Foxhounds are not fed as household pets, pack members being trencher-fed with horse flesh and an oatmeal mash called a 'pudding' The leaner hounds are led to the trough first, so that they may eat their fill, and then the remainder are led in. They are not fed the day before a hunt.

Origin and history
The Foxhound is descended from the heavier St Hubert Hounds, brought to England by the Norman invaders, and from the now extinct Talbot Hounds. The Ardennes Hounds derived their name of Hubertus Hounds from the Bishop of Liège who later became St Hubert, patron saint of all hunters.

The Foxhound is never exhibited at ordinary dog shows, but has its own events under the auspices, in the United Kingdom, of the Association of Masters of Foxhounds. 60▶

AMERICAN FOXHOUND

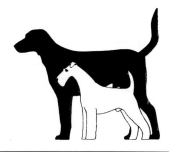

Good points
- *First-rate hunter*
- *Lively*
- *Full of stamina*
- *Friendly*

Take heed
- *Noisy*
- *Inclined to be disobedient*
- *This breed does not make a suitable pet*

The American Foxhound is a lighter, racier-looking dog than the English Foxhound. It is seen in the show ring in the USA.

Size
Height: dogs should not be under 56cm (22in) nor over 63.5cm (25in); bitches should not be under 53cm (21in) nor over 61cm (24in).

Exercise
Needs plenty of vigorous exercise.

Grooming
Use a hound glove.

Feeding
Foxhounds are not fed as household pets, pack members being trencher-fed with horse flesh and

Below: The American Foxhound, an agile and powerfully built hunter.

an oatmeal mash called a 'pudding' The leaner hounds are led to the trough first, so that they may eat their fill, and then the remainder are led in. They are not fed the day before a hunt.

Origin and history
The American Foxhound is believed to have been derived from a pack of Foxhounds taken from Britain to America by Robert Brooke in 1650. They are very fast, their quarry — the American red fox — being a speedier prey than its English counterpart. In about 1770, George Washington also imported Foxhounds from Great Britain and received the gift from Lafayette of some excellent French specimens in 1785. The French and English breeds were crossbred, producing the Virginia Hounds, which form today's American Foxhound. 60▶

SCANDINAVIAN HOUNDS

Smalands Hound

Dunker Hound

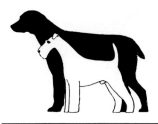

SMALANDS HOUND
(Smålandsstövare)

Good points
- *Keen hunting instinct*
- *Strong and sturdy*

Take heed
- *Not suitable as pet*

The Smalands Hound is, in company with the Hamilton Hound and Schiller Hound, one of the three oldest hunting varieties in Sweden. It is somewhat smaller than the other hunting varieties, strong, sturdy and able to cope with the dense forest that covers a large area of Smaland in southern Sweden. It is a born hunter of considerable strength and is not recommended as a house pet.

Size
About 49.5cm (19½in).

Grooming
Use a hound glove daily.

Feeding
One to 1½cans (376g, 13.3oz size) of a branded meaty product, with biscuit added in equal part by volume; or 3 cupfuls of a dry food, complete diet, mixed in the proportion of 1 cup of feed to ½ cup of hot or cold water.

Origin and history
This breed, although well known throughout Scandinavia, is little known elsewhere and is not recognized by the British or American Kennel Clubs. There are, however, numerous historical references to the breed in its country of origin, many of which refer to the breed's naturally short tail; it is never docked.

Baron von Essen is credited with perfecting the breed at the beginning of the 20th century through crossing the best of Swedish hounds with the Schiller Hound. The Smalands Hound was recognized by the Swedish KC in 1921.

DUNKER HOUND
(Norwegian Hound)

Good points
- *Excellent hunting dog*

Take heed
- *Not suitable as pet dog*

The Dunker Hound is a Norwegian variety, has considerable trekking ability and is a good retriever. It is popular in Sweden and throughout Scandinavia but is not recognized by the British or American Kennel Clubs. It has staying power rather than speed and is used to hunt the hare. The Dunker Hound is a strong dog, with a deep chest and long legs. It is both affectionate and trustworthy, but is not, however, recommended as a household pet.

Size
Height: 47-56cm (18½-22in).

Grooming
Use a hound glove. 60▶

SCANDINAVIAN HOUNDS

Schiller Hound

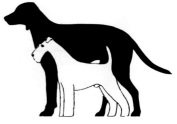

Finnish Hound

Feeding
One to 1½ cans (376g, 13.3oz size) of a branded meaty product, with biscuit added in equal part by volume; or 3 cupfuls of a dry food, complete diet, mixed in the proportion of 1 cup of feed to ½ cup of hot or cold water: or hound diet (see Foxhounds, page 29).

Origin and history
The Dunker takes its name from Wilhelm Dunker who, around the middle of the last century, mated his hound, renowned as a trekker and retriever, with the best bitches in order to perpetuate these hunting qualities. It is understood that crossing with the Hygen Hound took place at one time and an effort was made to register the progeny as Norwegian Beagles. However, the suggestion was rejected and the breeds have since gone their separate ways, both retaining considerable tracking ability. 60▶

SCHILLER HOUND (Schillerstövare)

Good points
● *Excellent hunting dog*

Take heed
● *Not recommended as a pet*

The Schiller Hound, like the Hamilton Hound, is one of Sweden's most popular hunting dogs, but is slightly shorter. It was evolved through crossing with hounds from Germany, Austria and Switzerland. The Schiller Hound is possibly the fastest of the Scandinavian hounds. It is also used for tracking.

Size
About 49.5-61cm (19½-24in).

Feeding
One to 1½ cans of a branded meaty product (376g, 13.3oz size), with biscuit added in equal part by volume; or 3 cupfuls of a dry food, complete diet, mixed in the proportion of 1 cup of feed to ½ cup of hot or cold water.

Grooming
Use a hound glove daily. 60▶

FINNISH HOUND
(Suomenajokoira)

Good points
● *Excellent hunting dog*

Take heed
● *Not recommended as a pet*

The most popular dog in Finland, used in its native land for hunting not only hare and fox, but also moose and lynx. The breed was established in the 19th century by a goldsmith named Tammelin, by careful crossing of English, German, Swiss and Scandinavian hounds. The Finnish Hound is good-natured and friendly but has a strong streak of independence.

Size
Height: dog, 54.5-61cm (21½-24in); bitch, 51-57cm (20-22½in).

Hygen Hound　　　　　　　　　　*Halden Hound*

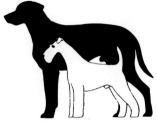

Feeding
As for other Scandinavian hounds.

Grooming
Use a hound glove daily. 60▶

HYGEN HOUND
(Hygenhund)

Good points
● *Excellent hunting dog*

Take heed
● *Not recommended as a pet*

The Hygen Hound excels in trekking and retrieving. It is a fine hunting dog, dignified and of equable temperament. It is, however, little known outside Scandinavia.

Size
About 61cm (24in).

Grooming
Used a hound glove daily.

Feeding
As for other Scandinavian hounds.

Origin and history
The breed takes its name from a Norwegian named Hygen who, in 1830, bred the now extinct Ringerike Hounds. The Hygen Hound emerged as a separate variety, and was then crossed with the Dunker, and an attempt was made to register the progeny under the name of Norwegian Beagles. This venture failed, and the breeds have gone their separate ways. Similarities in appearance remain but the Hygen

Hound is heavier and less poised than the Dunker, and it also retains the colour of the Ringerikes. 60▶

HALDEN HOUND
(Haldenstövare)

Good points
● *Excellent hunting dog*

Take heed
● *Not recommended as a pet*

This is a medium-sized hound, of considerable stamina, little known outside Scandinavia. It is a Norwegian breed named after the town of Halden. This gentle and affectionate hound has evolved through the crossing of Norwegian hounds by careful selection with hounds imported from Britain, Germany, France and, it is suggested, Russia.

Size
About 63.5cm (25in).

Feeding
As for other Scandinavian hounds.

Grooming
Use a hound glove daily. 60▶

NB. The Scandinavian hounds are not usually kept in packs. They hunt in forests, in countryside calling for a tallish hound with a good nose and able to give tongue loud and clear for the benefit of the following huntsmen.

LARGE MUNSTERLANDER

Good points
- *Affectionate*
- *Easily taught*
- *Good multi-purpose gundog*
- *Good house pet*
- *Loyal*
- *Trustworthy*

Take heed
- *Needs plenty of space for exercise*

The Large Munsterlander is officially recorded as the youngest pointing retriever gundog breed, but has been known in Germany for as long as all the other German gundog breeds. It resembles a setter in both build and coat, and has a head like that of a spaniel. It is a multi-purpose gundog, ideal for the rough shoot: it has an excellent nose and staying power, and works equally well on land or in water. It also makes an intelligent and likeable family pet.

Size
Height: dog approximately 61cm (24in); bitch approximately 58.5cm (23in). Weight: dog approximately 25-29.5kg (55-65lb); bitch approximately 25kg (55lb).

Exercise
This is an energetic dog needing plenty of exercise.

Below: The alert expression of the intelligent Large Munsterlander

Grooming
A daily brushing will be sufficient.

Feeding
One and a half to 2½ cans of branded dog food (376g, 13.3oz size) supplemented by biscuit in equal part by volume; or, if you prefer, 5 cupfuls of a dry food, complete diet, mixed as 1 cup of feed to ½ cup of hot or cold water.

Origin and history
In bygone days, the best working dogs were mated to the best working bitches, with little regard to colour, breeding or coat texture. Early in the 19th century, however, people became breed- and colour-conscious and records of the best dogs were kept. So it was with the Large Munsterlander, which was then classed as a Long-haired German Pointer.

When the German Kennel Club was founded and the general stud book came into operation, only brown and white Long-haired German Pointers were permitted registration. The litters containing 'odd-coloured' puppies were frequently given away, finding their way into the hands of farmers and gamekeepers, who were delighted to have such well-bred dogs that would work. They were not bothered by the dogs' lack of colour or of registration. This was fortunate, for it resulted in the saving of the breed now known as the Large Munsterlander.

The Small Munsterlander (or Moorland Spaniel) is a lighter dog, 43-56cm (17-22in) tall. 61▶

DRENTSE PARTRIDGE DOG *(Drentse Patrijshond, Dutch Partridge Dog)*

Good points
- *Affectionate*
- *Equable temperament*
- *Excellent gundog*
- *Easy to train*
- *Intelligent*
- *Good house pet*

Take heed
- *No drawbacks known*

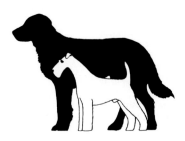

The Drentse Partridge Dog is little known outside Holland. This is a pity, because not only is it an attractive dog — something like the Springer Spaniel in appearance — but it also admirably combines the role of all-purpose gundog with that of an affectionate family pet. It will point and retrieve, and has been a successful competitor in Field Trials in its homeland.

Despite its descriptive name, the Drentse Partridge Dog is a dog that is able to work all kinds of game and is also able to retrieve pheasant and hare.

The breed, which is at home on either land or in water, and has an acute sense of smell, is depicted in a great many Dutch paintings, most notable of which is a fine head study by Henrick Goltzius (1558-1617).

Although little known outside its native Holland, it is possible that the Drentse Partridge Dog has been around considerably longer than the 300 years with which it is generally credited. Indeed some experts, including the late Harry Glover, say that it represents the very early type of half Spaniel, half Setter that was possibly the ancestor of many modern gundogs such as the Irish Setter.

While similar in appearance to the English Springer Spaniel there is also something of the rarely seen German Langhaar (Longhair) in its physical make-up, the main differences being the Partridge Dog's short head and the fact that its muzzle is square without being weighty. It has a similar scenting ability.

Certainly, the Drentse Partridge dog is a fine looking animal. Like so many gundogs, its gentle and obedient nature combines ideally the role of sportsman's dog and children's pet.

It has a basically white coat with orange markings, is well proportioned and has a body which is longer than its height at the withers. It has amber eyes.

With increased importations, hopefully we shall see more examples in the show ring.

Size
Height about 58.5-61cm (23-24in).

Exercise
Needs plenty of exercise in open spaces to stay healthy.

Grooming
Regular brushing will maintain the coat in good condition.

Feeding
About 1½-2½ cans (376g, 13.3oz size) of a branded meaty product, with biscuit added in equal part by volume; or 5 cupfuls of a dry food, complete diet, mixed in the proportion of 1 cup to ½ cup of water.

Origin and history
The Drentse Partridge Dog, or Patrijshond, comes from the Drentse district of north-east Holland, where it has existed for at least 300 years, no doubt having evolved through early crossings with long-haired German sporting breeds. It is an accomplished wildfowler, and obviously justifies more widespread popularity. 61▶

PHARAOH HOUND

Good points
- *Striking appearance*
- *Affectionate*
- *Intelligent*
- *Excellent hunter*
- *Full of fun*
- *Good with children*

Take heed
- *Not suitable for town life*
- *Wary of strangers*

The Pharaoh Hound is the oldest domesticated dog in recorded history. Two hounds hunting gazelle are depicted on a circular disc dating back to around 4000 BC, certainly before the First Dynasty.

The dog, and particularly the hunting dog, played an intimate part in the daily life of kings and nobles in Ancient Egypt. It is therefore not surprising to find them frequently depicted in the reliefs carved on the tomb walls of these men.

The Pharaoh Hound is a medium-sized hound, elegant, powerful and swift. It is intelligent, affectionate and full of fun; also very good with children, but a little diffident at first with strangers. Out hunting it is keen and fast. Unlike the Greyhound it hunts by both scent and sight.

Size
Height: dog ideally 56-63.5cm (22-25in); bitch ideally 53-61cm (21-24in). Overall balance must be maintained.

Exercise
This is a breed that needs plenty of exercise. It is unsuitable for town or apartment living.

Grooming
The silky, smooth coat needs little attention for a smart appearance.

Feeding
This is a hardy and healthy breed, yet on the island of Gozo (near Malta), to which it is believed the Pharaoh Hound was brought by Phoenicians, it was fed almost entirely on a meat-free diet of soup and goat's milk. Nowadays it enjoys a more traditional canine diet, but care must be taken that it does not become over-weight.

Recommended would be 1-1½ cans of a branded, meaty product (376g, 13.3oz size), with biscuit added in equal part by volume; or 3 cupfuls of a complete, dry food, mixed in the proportion of 1 cup of feed to ½ cup of hot or cold water. Increase rations if working.

Origin and history
It is thought that the Phoenicians took these hounds with them when they settled on Malta and Gozo, and that the preservation of the breed, which has changed little in 5000 years, can be accredited to Malta, where it is known to have existed for over 2000 years. In Malta, Pharaohs are bred for rabbit hunting and are known by the Maltese as 'kelb-tal-fenek' (rabbit dog).

In 1935 the Harvard-Boston expedition, under Dr George Reisner, working in the great cemetery west of the Pyramid of Cheops at Giza, found an inscription recording the burial of a dog named Abuwtiyuw. The burial was carried out with all the ritual ceremonies of a great man of Egypt, by order of the kings of Upper and Lower Egypt.

Like other Egyptian nobles, the dog was in constant attendance, a daily fact in the life of the king; and when it died, the monarch ordered that it be buried ceremonially in a tomb of its own. 61▶

IBIZAN HOUND

Good points
- *Excellent with children*
- *Good gundog*
- *Kind disposition*
- *Seldom fights*
- *Wonderful house pet*

Take heed
- *Has acute hearing so must not be shouted at*
- *Sensitive and easily hurt*

The Ibizan Hound is a kind dog loved by children, in whom it seems to inspire confidence. It is easily hurt, however, and due to its acute hearing must not be shouted at or its spirit can be crushed. It has great stamina and can, according to the natives of Ibiza, hunt by day or by night, singly or in pairs. But it is not a dog to go off on its own and not return. These dogs seldom fight, and have to be pushed to do so. They willingly retrieve and are often taken hunting on the island without guns. It is said that a pair can catch 1000 rabbits in a day. They are useful as gundogs, and make wonderful house pets.

Size
Weight 22.2-22.7kg (49-50lb); height 56-71cm (22-28in), for a dog, less for a bitch.

Exercise
It would be unkind to keep this hound in a confined space, for it is a tireless dog, able to retrieve and to jump great heights. It is an excellent companion for a sportsman. It must not be kennelled; ideally it should be kept as a companion in the home.

Grooming
The Ibizan needs a good brush every day but is not difficult to maintain in good condition.

Feeding
Recommended would be 1-1½ cans (376g, 13.3oz size) of a branded meaty product, with biscuit added in equal part by volume; or 3 cupfuls of a dry food, complete diet, mixed in the proportion of 1 cup of feed to ½ cup of hot or cold water. The addition of raw fish and fruit to the diet of the Ibizan is beneficial.

Origin and history
We know that hounds like the Ibizan were owned by the ancient pharaohs of Egypt, because hunting dogs of this type were drawn on rock, stone and papyrus as early as 3000 BC. Indeed, bones of similar hunting dogs have been found from about 4770 BC. The dogs of the pharaohs probably spread through trade to neighbouring lands. On the invasion of Egypt by the Romans, their neighbours the Carthaginians and the Phoenicians were driven out to the island of Ibiza in the 9th century BC, where they lived for about a century; but the hounds that they brought with them remained on Ibiza for the next 3000 years. Although some fine hounds have recently been taken from Ibiza to Majorca, the purest hounds are still found on Ibiza, retaining all the colours shown in the Egyptian drawings, i.e. spotted red and lion on white, or any of these as a single colour.

The Ibizan Hound is a relative newcomer to America. The offspring of imports made in 1956, together with the pups of subsequent imports, formed the basis of a thriving breeding population. The aim of all breeders is to maintain the fine qualities of the original island dogs. The AKC approved the breed for showing purposes in 1979. 61 ▶

SALUKI (Gazelle Hound)

Good points
- *Excellent guard*
- *Good companion*
- *Healthy*
- *Intelligent*
- *Odour-free*
- *Reliable with childen*

Take heed
- *Strong hunting instincts*
- *Needs plenty of exercise*

The Saluki and the horse are prized Arab possessions. the Saluki being capable of great speed and able to keep pace with the fleet-footed Arab stallions. It is still used in the Middle East for hunting the gazelle, but in the West it is kept mainly as an elegant companion, pet and show dog. It is intelligent and somewhat aloof, but is a faithful, gentle companion and trustworthy with children. Care must be taken, particularly in country areas, that the Saluki is kept under control; despite its domestic role, it retains very strong hunting instincts.

Size
Height of dog should average 58.5-71cm (23-28in), bitch slightly smaller.

Exercise
Salukis need plenty of exercise, and ownership should not be contemplated by those without a large garden or other exercise area.

Grooming
Brush daily with a soft brush, and use a hound glove. Combing of ear and tail fringes may also be necessary, especially if the owner intends to enter the beautiful Saluki for a dog show.

Feeding
One to 1½ cans (376g, 13.3oz) of a branded meaty product, with biscuit added in equal part by volume; or 3 cupfuls of a dry food, complete diet, mixed in the proportion of 1 cup of feed to ½ cup of hot or cold water.

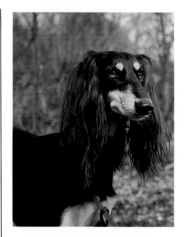

Above: The Saluki has strong hunting instincts and must be kept under control in country areas.

Origin and history
The Saluki is one of the most ancient breeds of dog and, like the Afghan and Greyhound, is a sight hound that derives from the Middle East. The Saluki is said to take its name from Saluk in the Yemen, but its likeness is portrayed on the tombs of the Egyptian Pharaohs.

The breed did not gain recognition by the American Kennel Club until 1927. In Britain it was known long before, for a litter bred in London Zoo in 1836 was shown as the 'Persian Greyhound'. The breed was recognized by the British Kennel Club in 1922 and has excelled as a show dog. The Sloughi, one of the rarest sighthounds, closely resembles the Saluki, but is short-coated.

AFGHAN HOUND

Good points
- *Loyal and affectionate*
- *Good with children who do not tease*

Take heed
- *Must have space — not suitable for apartments*
- *Needs daily grooming*
- *Must have firm, loving handling*
- *Can be fiery tempered*

The Afghan is dignified, aloof and fond of comfort. Though it enjoys nothing more than surveying the scene from a cosy armchair, the Afghan is not the ideal choice for apartment dwellers or even those with a small house and garden. For despite its beautiful house manners, the Afghan is basically a hunting dog, warmly affectionate to its owners and usually trustworthy with children, but independent in character and often quite fiery in temper, particularly in adolescence.

It is impossible to show an Afghan too much affection, and it shouldn't be bullied. But it is important to maintain superiority from the first, especially during showing and training sessions, or later you may suffer the indignity, and physical near-impossibility, of publicly wrestling with a powerful creature armed with a mouthful of large teeth.

Size
Ideal height: dog 68.5-73.5cm (27-29in), bitch approximately 5-7.5cm (2-3in) smaller.

Exercise
Afghans need free running to keep fit and happy; their original task was to hunt wolves and gazelles in the deserts of Afghanistan, so a stroll in the park or a run up and down a suburban garden will not be enough to subdue their boundless energy. A puppy, from the first should be allowed unrestricted exercise in its waking hours. This should be in a safe enclosed place. An adult should have a minimum of half an hour's free galloping a day, as well as disciplined walking on the lead.

Grooming
Daily grooming is vitally important to prevent the dog's thick coat from matting; the well-groomed Afghan is a delight to behold, the neglected specimen an abomination. Indeed, this breed is definitely not for those with little time on their hands for grooming and exercising.

The only type of brush capable of getting through an Afghan's coat is one with an air cushion behind the tufts. The best of all is a Mason Pearson real bristle — made for humans, and expensive. The nylon version is cheaper but remember to use a coat lubricant with this, otherwise static electricity will build up and cause the hair to become brittle. An air-cushioned brush with steel pins is excellent, and is not expensive.

Feeding
Recommended would be 1½-2½ cans (376g, 13.3oz size) of a branded meaty product, with biscuit added in equal part by volume; or 5 cupfuls of a dry food, complete diet, mixed in the proportion of 1 cup of feed to ½ cup of hot or cold water.

Origin and history
The Afghan is an ancient breed reputed to have been among those creatures taken into the Ark by Noah, and, to quote the book

Above: The Afghan Hound must surely be the most elegant and glamorous dog in the world.

Champion Dogs of the World, 'even if one rejects this claim it still remains virtually certain that some sort of Afghan existed thousands of years ago in the Middle East'. Present-day experts believe that it was crossed with the Saluki.

A papyrus found in Sinai dated *c.* 3000 BC was, from early translations, thought to refer to a Cynocephalus, or monkey-faced hound; this could have been the forerunner of the Afghan, which because of its facial resemblance is often called a 'monkey dog'. However, later work on the translation confirmed belief that it referred not to a dog but to a hound-faced baboon.

At any rate a Greyhound-like dog was destined to find its way, perhaps through Persia, to Afghanistan, where it grew a long, shaggy coat for protection against the harsh climate and found favour with the royal and aristocratic families of that land.

The first Afghan Hound Breed Club was formed in the United Kingdom in 1926. The AKC adopted a breed standard in the same year, but a totally new and original one was accepted in 1948. 62▶

GREYHOUND

One of the most ancient breeds and, some say, the most misunderstood, for although built for speed and used for racing and coursing, the Greyhound is basically lazy. It adapts well to life as a family pet, and will enjoy nothing better than lazing on a settee or mattress, which is what it will have done for many hours when living in racing kennels. It is a good-natured, friendly and affectionate dog, and is very gentle with children.

Size
Dog 71-76cm (28-30in); bitch 68.5-71cm (27-28in). There is no standard desired weight.

Exercise
Three or four short walks every day will be sufficient. Although the Greyhound must never be exercised off the lead in a public place, it will enjoy the opportunity to run free in open country, away from sheep and other livestock. It is a highly sensitive creature, and will learn to respond quickly to the tone of voice, which helps greatly in obedience training.

Grooming
Daily use of a hound glove will keep the coat shining.

Feeding
A retired Greyhound is like every other dog in that it responds best to a regular routine, especially where feeding and exercise are concerned. During their racing careers they are fed twice daily, in the early morning and in mid-afternoon, and exercised four times a day. There is no need to continue this routine once the Greyhound has settled in a new home, but it is kind to allow it to adapt gradually to its new lifestyle.

The canned food requirement for a Greyhound is between 1½ and 2½ cans of branded dog food (376g, 13.3oz size) per day and this, or 340-454g (12-16oz) of minced or chopped meat, should be mixed with 284-454g (10-16oz) of biscuit meal and moistened with bone stock, for Greyhounds are used to sloppier food than most breeds. They should also be pampered with a thick slice of brown bread crumbled into 0.28l (½pt) of milk at breakfast time, and have a small drink of milk with two large-sized dog biscuits at bedtime.

Health care
A retired Greyhound may at first be restless in its new surroundings. It must be remembered that the home is a very different environment from a racing track, and it is unlikely that a retired racing Greyhound, when it leaves the track, will have seen home appliances such as television sets.

Origin and history
The Greyhound is a pure breed: that is, it has not evolved from crossings with other types. Indeed, it seems unlikely that this breed has altered materially since early Egyptian times, as proved by a carving of a Greyhound in an Egyptian tomb in the Nile Valley, circa 4000 BC. 62▶

AIREDALE

Good points
- *Attractive, sporty appearance*
- *Faithful (if formidable) guard*
- *Good with children*

Take heed
- *That hard, wiry coat ought to be hand stripped*
- *If it gets into a fight, you could end up with the other chap's veterinarian's bill!*

The Airedale is the king of the terriers and the largest of the terrier group. It is a splendid-looking animal with plenty of stamina, and combines ideally the roles of family pet and guard.

Prior to the First World War, the Airedale worked as a patrol dog with dock and railway police. It served during the war in the Russian Army and the British Army. It also worked for the Red Cross, locating the wounded and carrying messages. Indeed, at that time its abilities as a messenger and guard were considered superior to those of the German Shepherd Dog.

Size
Approximately 25kg (55lb). Height: dogs 61cm (24in) at the shoulder, bitches slightly less.

Exercise
One of the useful features about this dog is that although large it will adapt easily to living in a reasonably confined space, provided that it has at least two good 20-minute walks and an off-the-lead run every day. Alternatively, it will be in its element running with horses in the country and squelching, with wagging tail, through muddy fields.

Grooming
The Airedale needs a daily grooming with a stiff brush, and if you plan to enter the dog in the show ring it is essential that its coat is regularly hand stripped. Ask the breeder to show you how this is done and don't be ashamed if you eventually resort to having the job done by a skilled canine beautician. If you do not plan to show, you need have your Airedale stripped only in spring and summer for coolness and neatness, but allow it to keep its thick coat for winter protection.

Feeding
The Airedale needs at least 1-1½ cans (376g, 13.3oz size) of a branded meaty dog food, or the fresh meat equivalent, every day, plus a generous supply of biscuit meal. It will also appreciate the occasional large dog biscuit.

Watch the Airedale's weight and, if it shows signs of becoming too heavy, reduce the supply of biscuit meal. Its girth will depend on how active a life the dog leads.

Origin and history
The Airedale is named after the valley of Aire in Yorkshire from which its ancestors came. It was originally called the Waterside, or working terrier. The forerunner of the present-day Airedale was kept for vermin control by Yorkshire gamekeepers and it was probably crossed with the Otterhound.

In the late 1800s the Fox Terrier enjoyed immense popularity, and much thought and care went into the breeding and development of this bigger terrier as an attractive and, at the same time, useful dog. It was soon adopted as a companion, but — when given the chance — can still prove itself as an expert ratter and ducker. It can also be trained to the gun. 63▶

DOBERMANN (Dobermann Pinscher; Doberman)

Good points
- *Brave*
- *Loyal*
- *Ideal guard*

Take heed
- *Stands aloof from those outside the family circle*
- *Likely to win any battle*
- *If kennelled outside, needs heated, draught-proof kennels*

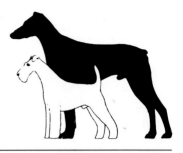

The Dobermann is a strong, alert guard that will enjoy the comforts of its master's fireside and protect him and his family with its life. It is unlikely to have to give its life, however, for the Dobermann generally gets the better of any opponent and is one of the best guard dogs in the world. It is an aloof animal that takes its responsibilities seriously, is skilled at tracking, and makes a fine police dog.

Size
Ideal height at withers: dog 68.5cm (27in); bitch 65cm (25½in). Considerable deviation from this ideal to be discouraged.

Exercise
Certainly at least 40 minutes each day, which must include a 10-minute off-the-lead run in an unrestricted open space.

Grooming
The Dobermann, with its short coat, needs little grooming other than a daily rub down with Turkish towelling to remove loose hairs.

Feeding
Recommended would be 1½-2½ cans (376g, 13.3oz size) of a branded, meaty product, with biscuit added in equal part by volume; or 5 cupfuls of a dry food, complete diet, mixed in the proportion of 1 cupful of feed to ½ cupful of hot or cold water. Yeast tablets are beneficial at meal-times, especially during winter; also cod liver oil. These dogs fare well on raw meat, which keeps them in excellent condition.

Above: The Dobermann—a noble breed renowned as a guard dog.

Origin and history
Louis Dobermann of Apolda, in Thuringia, Germany, was a tax collector during the 1880s. Having a penchant for fierce dogs, he decided to breed the ideal animal to accompany him on his rounds. It was a relatively easy task for him, as he was keeper of the local dog pound, with access to numerous strays. He had in mind a medium- to large-sized dog, which must be short-coated (thus easily maintained).

The existing German Pinscher was considered to be both aggressive and alert, so it was around this breed that Louis Dobermann founded his stock, introducing the the Rottweiler—a dog with great stamina and tracking ability—and, it is believed, the Manchester Terrier, which at that time was a much larger animal; no doubt it is from the Manchester that the Dobermann obtained its gleaming coat and black and tan markings. Possibly the Pointer was also used.

63▶

HUNGARIAN VIZSLA

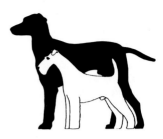

Good points
- *Distinguished appearance*
- *First-class gundog*
- *Clean*
- *Steady temperament*
- *Intelligent*
- *Easy to train*
- *Makes an excellent family pet*

Take heed
- *No drawbacks known*

The Vizsla is Hungary's national dog and one of the purest breeds in the world. It is an excellent all-purpose gundog, with a keen nose, and well able to point, set and retrieve. Despite its hunting abilities it adapts happily to life as a family pet, and its temperament is sound.

Size
Height at withers: dog 57-63.5cm (22½-25in); bitch 53-60cm (21-23½in). Weight: 22-30kg (48½-66lb).

Exercise
Needs plenty of vigorous exercise.

Grooming
Regular brushing will keep the coat in a healthy condition.

Feeding
Recommended would be 1½-2½ cans (376g, 13.3oz size) of a branded meaty product, with biscuit added in equal part by volume; or 5 cupfuls of a dry food, complete diet, mixed in the proportion of 1 cup of feed to ½ cup of hot or cold water.

Origin and history
The Hungarian Vizsla was no doubt developed by the Magyar nobles and great care has been taken to avoid introducing new blood. It is a pure breed of outstanding ability and quality. 70▶

Below: The Hungarian Vizsla is a pure breed of distinguished appearance that makes an excellent gundog and sound family pet.

BEARDED COLLIE

Good points
- *Devoted pet*
- *Good with children*
- *Intelligent*
- *Natural herder*
- *Playful*
- *Easily trained*
- *Beautiful show dog*

Take heed
- *Needs plenty of exercise*

The Bearded Collie is not so well known as other Collies in Britain, and was almost extinct after the Second World War. Now, however, numbers of this delightful breed are increasing. It is a lovable dog, ideally suited for family life, but retaining its herding capabilities. It is easily trained and reliable with children, and proves a willing, lively playmate.

Size
Ideal height at the shoulder: dog 53-56cm (21-22in), bitch 51-53cm (20-21in).

Exercise
Not suitable for a confined existence. Needs plenty of exercise, including off-the-lead runs.

Grooming
Daily brushing. Bathing and chalking are necessary for show.

Feeding
One to 1½ cans (376g, 13.3oz size) of a branded meaty product, with biscuit added in equal part by volume; or 3 cupfuls of a dry food, complete diet, mixed in the proportion of 1 cup of feed to ½ cup of hot or cold water.

Origin and history
The lovable Beardie bears a keen resemblance to the Old English Sheepdog, or Bobtail, and is reckoned to be one of the oldest herding dogs in Scotland. It is said to be of Polish origin, being derived from purebred Polish Lowland Sheepdogs — two bitches and a dog were exchanged on a trading

Above: A Bearded Collie with her puppy.

voyage to Scotland in 1514, for a ram and a ewe. It has also been said to have Hungarian blood.

Luckily the survival of the breed was assured when Mrs G. Willison, of the former Bothkennar Kennels, acquired a Beardie bitch puppy (then without pedigree) in 1944, and, after a fruitless search for a Beardie dog, found one playing with its owners on the beach at Hove, Sussex. They were willing to sell and from this pair, 'Jeannie' and 'Bailie', all to-day's Beardies are descended.

A dog that bears a fairly strong resemblance to the Beardie is the Dutch Schapendoes, which has Beardie blood in its veins, as well probably as that of the Bergamasco, Puli and Briard. It is a popular sheepdog, guard and house-dog in Holland, but is little known in other countries. 63▶

ROUGH COLLIE (Rough-haired Collie)

Good points
- *Attractive appearance*
- *Affectionate*
- *Easily trained*
- *Excellent pet*
- *Loves children*
- *Loyal*
- *Good guard dog*

Take heed
- *Not too keen on strangers*

No breed causes so much consternation to buyers and those giving breed information as the Collie. People tend to have a fixed idea of the type of Collie they want, be it Rough, Smooth, Border, Old English or Bearded. The Smooth Collie is identical to the Rough Collie except in coat. There are also long-haired and wire-haired varieties. If it's a dog like the film star 'Lassie' that you want, you *are* thinking of a Rough Collie, sometimes erroneously called Scottish Collie; the Sheltie, or Shetland, is a Rough Collie in miniature.

The Rough Collie makes an ideal family pet, being biddable, affectionate and loyal. It is hardy and, despite its thick coat, relatively simple to groom.

Size
Height at shoulder: dog 56-61cm (22-24in); bitch 51-56cm (20-22in). Weight: dog 20.5-29.5kg (45-65lb); bitch 18.1-25kg (40-55lb).

Exercise
Normal daily exercise with off-the-lead runs when possible.

Grooming
Daily brushing. Don't be afraid to vacuum clean with the smallest brush, if it gets muddy. But get the dog accustomed to the noise of the machine first.

Feeding
Recommended would be 1½-2½ cans (376g, 13.3oz size) of a branded meaty product, with biscuit added in equal part by volume; or 5 cupfuls of a dry food, complete diet, mixed in the proportion of 1 cup of feed to ½ cup of hot or cold water.

Origin and history
The Rough Collie is generally spoken of as a Scottish breed. In fact, its ancestors were introduced into England and Scotland from Iceland 400 years ago. But it was as guardians of the flock that they acquired their name in Scotland, where sheep with black faces and legs were known as colleys. Queen Victoria kept a Rough Collie at Balmoral in 1860, and in the same year a breed member was exhibited in a Birmingham show. 63▶

Below: The beautiful Rough Collie, an aristocratic-looking breed with a friendly nature, lively spirit and hardy constitution.

GERMAN SHORT-HAIRED POINTER

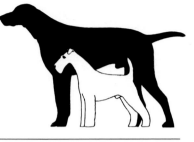

Good points
- *Easily trained*
- *Equable temperament*
- *Excellent gundog*
- *Good with children*
- *Makes a good household pet*
- *Obedient*
- *Good watchdog*

Take heed
- *Needs plenty of exercise*

The German Short-haired Pointer is a good all-round sporting dog, and affectionate and good with children. It is, however, happiest when in the wide open spaces, and is excellent at working wildfowl and most types of game. It is a first-rate swimmer.

Size
Dog 58.5-63.5cm (23-25in); bitch 53-58.5cm (21-23in).

Exercise
Needs plenty of exercise.

Grooming
Brush the coat regularly.

Feeding
Recommended would be 1½-2½ cans (376g, 13.3oz size) of a branded meaty product, with biscuit added in equal part by volume; or 5 cupfuls of a dry food, complete diet, mixed in the proportion of 1 cup of feed to ½ cup of hot or cold water.

Origin and history
The German Short-haired Pointer is of Spanish origin, bred from dogs imported into Germany and crossed with local hounds and, probably, with the English Foxhound for speed, the Bloodhound for nose, and the English Pointer to retain its pointing ability. 64 ▶

Below: A noble, steady dog showing power, endurance and speed, the German Short-haired Pointer can work in the water as well as on land. Given plenty of exercise, it will adapt to a family life at home.

POINTER

Good points
- Equable temperament
- Obedient
- Good with children
- Easily trained
- Excellent gundog
- Makes a good household pet
- Successful show dog

Take heed
- Needs plenty of exercise

The Pointer is famed for its classic pose 'pointing' with its nose and tail in the direction of the game that has been shot. It is a friendly dog, and makes an ideal household pet, getting on well with other animals. and children. But it does need a generous amount of exercise to really thrive.

Size
Desirable height: dog 63.5-68.5cm (25-27in); bitch 61-66cm (24-26in).

Exercise
Needs plenty of exercise.

Grooming
Brush the coat regularly.

Feeding
Recommended would be 1½-2½ cans (376g, 13.3oz size) of a branded meaty product, with biscuit added in equal part by volume; or 5 cupfuls of a dry food, complete diet, mixed in the proportion of 1 cup of feed to ½ cup of hot or cold water.

Origin and history
There is some controversy as to whether the Pointer originated in Spain, or was produced in Britain through crossings of Bloodhounds, Foxhounds and Greyhounds. A great authority on the breed, William Arkwright of Sutton Scarsdale, England, spent his life travelling the world to check on the history and development of the breed. He believed that it originated in the East, found its way to Italy, then to Spain (where it developed its classic head) and thence to England and South America. *Arkwright on Pointers* is still the bible of the breed. 64▶

Below: The Pointer conveys the impression of strength and endurance.

IRISH SETTER (Red Setter)

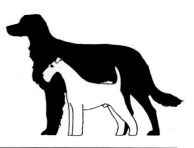

Good points
- Affectionate
- Beautiful
- Excellent with children
- Hunting ability
- Successful show dog

Take heed
- Lively
- No good as a guard; it loves everybody!

The Irish Setter is a first-class gundog that combines this work admirably with the role of family pet. It is happiest as a housedog and has great need of affection, which it returns a hundredfold. It is intelligent and utterly reliable with children. It is, however, high spirited and lively and should not be confined in close quarters or kept by those who cannot provide adequate exercise. It often strikes up a good relationship with horses.

Size
The Americans look for a tall dog, 63.5-68.5cm (25-27in) high, but in Britain no height is specified.

Exercise
An exuberant dog that needs lots of exercise, either working or running in the wide open spaces.

Left and below: Supremely elegant, the Irish Setter is a champion pet, show breed and working gundog.

Grooming
That luxurious coat will need regular brushing to keep it looking glossy. Keep the ears clean.

Feeding
Recommended would be 1½-2½ cans (376g, 13.3oz size) of a branded meaty product, with biscuit added in equal part by volume; or 5 cupfuls of a dry food, complete diet, mixed in the proportion of 1 cup of feed to ½ cup of hot or cold water.

Origin and history
The Irish Setter has evolved from the crossing of Irish Water Spaniels, Springer Spaniels, the Spanish Pointer and English and Gordon Setters, its name being settled by the Ulster Irish Setter Club in 1876. Synonymous with the breed is the name of Edward Laverack who, prior to his death in 1877, spent almost a lifetime improving the breed. 64▶

ENGLISH SETTER

Good points
- *Adaptable*
- *Beautiful*
- *Can live in house or kennel*
- *Reliable gundog*

Take heed
- *Not a loner; thrives in company of humans or of other dogs*
- *Needs plenty of exercise*

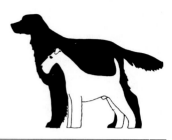

The English Setter is the most distinctive of the three Setter varieties, Irish, Gordon and English. It has a gentle nature that makes it the ideal companion for children, at the same time being an excellent gundog. As it needs lots of exercise, it is not a suitable companion for a flat dweller. It also requires a fair amount of grooming.

Size
Weight: dog 27.2-30kg (60-66lb); bitch 25.4-28.1kg (56-62lb). Height: dog 65-68.5cm (25½-27in); bitch 61-63.5cm (24-25in).

Exercise
Needs at least 10 minutes of exercise a day as a 3-month-old pup and a hour in adulthood to keep it in top condition.

Grooming
You will need trimming scissors and a fine steel comb for daily grooming, also a good stiff brush for the coat. Take care that the feathering on the legs does not become tangled. The silky hair under the ears should be removed and also hair under the throat and below the ear down to the breast bone. Care must also be taken to remove hair that forms between the dog's pads. Any straggly hairs have to be plucked from the body before the dog goes into the show ring. The English Setter is always bathed before a show, and the coat combed flat when it is dry. American competitors are trimmed more heavily than those exhibited in the United Kingdom.

Origin and history
It is generally agreed that the English Setter evolved from spaniels. Credit for the breed is given to Edward Laverack (1815-1877) who in his work *The Setter* wrote: 'this breed is but a Spaniel improved'. The Setting Spaniel, accepted by many modern authorities as the fore-runner of the English Setter, was used as far back as the 16th century for setting partridges and quails. Through interbreeding, Laverack affected the strain so that it acquired not only the standard of excellence in the 19th century but that on which the present-day English Setter was built. To quote Sylvia Bruce Wilmore writing in *Dog News* magazine: 'About the time the Laverack strain of English Setter was at its zenith, Mr R.L. Purcell Llewellin purchased a number of Mr Laverack's best Show dogs of the pure Dash-Moll and Dash-Hill Laverack blood. He crossed these with entirely new blood which he obtained in the North of England represented by Mr Slatter's and Sir Vincent Corbet's strain, since referred to as the Duke-Kate-Rhoebe. The Llewellin strain of English Setter became immensely popular at the turn of the century, their reputation spreading to the United States and Canada where they dominated field trials for a quarter of a century, thus firmly establishing the line of breed in America. 64▶

GORDON SETTER

Good points
- *Affectionate*
- *Intelligent*
- *Equable temperament*
- *Tireless worker*
- *Excellent gundog*
- *Good with children*

Take heed
- *Not suitable for a guard dog*
- *Needs plenty of exercise*

The Gordon Setter is a fine gun-dog, a bird-finding dog, used to silent trekking. It does not fit the role of guard, although it will not accept strangers as readily as the Irish Setter, which could well lick the face of a burglar while presenting him with some item 'retrieved' from its mistress's wardrobe.

The Gordon makes an excellent family pet and is trustworthy with children. It does enjoy an active working life, however, and is not really suitable for apartments.

Size
Shoulder height for dog, 66cm (26in), weight about 29.5kg (65lb); bitch, 62cm (24½in), weight about 25.4kg (56lb).

Exercise
Ensure that it has plenty of exercise.

Below: The Gordon Setter is a strong gundog and friendly pet.

Grooming
Regular brushing, and monthly nail clipping.

Feeding
Recommended would be 1½-2½ cans (376g, 13.3oz size) of a branded meaty product, with biscuit added in equal part by volume; or 5 cupfuls of a dry food, complete diet, mixed in the proportion of 1 cup of feed to ½ cup of hot or cold water.

Origin and history
The Gordon is a true Scot, bred at Gordon Castle, Banffshire, the seat of the Duke of Richmond and Gordon. It is the only native Scottish gundog and was originally known as the Gordon Castle Setter. Credit must go to the 4th Duke of Richmond and Gordon for establishing the breed in the late 1770s, using probably the Collie and the Bloodhound. 64▶

BELGIAN SHEPHERD DOG

Good points
- *Alert and agile*
- *Excellent guard*
- *Intelligent*
- *Physically robust*

Take heed
- *Best suited to the open spaces, so won't take kindly to apartment living*
- *Needs firm but kind handling*

There are four types of Belgian Shepherd Dog—the Groenendael, the Laekenois, the Malinois and the Tervueren—all of which are similar to the German Shepherd.

Basically, they are hunting and herding dogs, but they have also served as Red Cross messengers in war-time, are vigilant guards and kindly protectors of children.

Size
The desired height for the dog is 61-66cm (24-26in) and for the bitch 56-61cm (22-24in). This applies to all four types.

Exercise
The Belgian Shepherd Dog is a working dog that excels in defending master and property. It is oblivious to bad weather, and enjoys being out of doors, so adequate exercise is vital.

Grooming
Little grooming is needed other than a good surface brushing. Bathing is not recommended, even for exhibition, unless the dog has got its coat into a filthy condition. As it has a double coat, combing out the under-coat will result in a dog with only half a coat.

Feeding
The Belgian Shepherd Dog should be fed similarly to other dogs of its size. Daily rations might be 1½ to 2 cans of branded dog food (376g, 13.3oz side), with an equal volume of biscuits, or 5 cupfuls of a dry food, complete diet, mixed in the proportion of 1 cup to ½ cup of hot or cold water.

Origin and history
At the end of the 19th century there were Shepherd Dog varieties of all colours and sizes in Belgium, but in about 1890, Monsieur Rose of the Café du Groenendael discovered a black, long-coated bitch among one of his litters. Later, he bought a similar dog from a Monsieur Bernaert and, by selective breeding and strict culling, eventually produced the Groenendael.

The origin of the modern Belgian Shepherd Dog dates from 1891, when a collection of shepherd dogs of all colours and sizes was gathered at the Brussels Veterinary University. It was decided to recognize three varieties: the rough-coated black; the smooth-coated fawn with black mask; and the wire-haired darkish grey. Since then there have been various additions to and subtractions from these types, but they have now been settled into four varieties: the Groenendael (long-coated black); the Tervueren (long-coated other than black); the Malinois (smooth-coated); and the Laekenois, or de Laeken (wire-coated).

It should be mentioned that in America only the Groenendael is known as the Belgian Shepherd Dog or Belgian Sheepdog; the Malinois and the Tervueren are registered as separate breeds, and the Laekenois—the rarest of the four—is not recognized. Incidentally, the breeds are known in America as the Belgian Malinois and the Belgian Tervuren, the latter with a different spelling. 65▶

HOLLANDSE HERDER (Dutch Shepherd Dog)

Good points
- *Excellent guard*
- *Hardy*
- *Intelligent*
- *Alert and active*
- *Sound temperament*
- *Faithful*
- *Easy to train*

Take heed
- *No drawbacks known*

The Hollandse Herder was bred in Holland as a sheepdog, but nowadays is kept mainly as a companion and guard. It is relatively unknown outside its native country, where it is used as a police dog, as a guide dog for the blind (seeing eye dog) and occasionally for farmyard duties. It comes in three coat types: shorthair, long-hair and wire-hair. The long-haired variety is almost extinct and the wire-hair is not commonly seen; the short-hair type is the one most widely known.

Size
Height at the withers: dog 58.5-63.5cm (23-25in); bitch 54.5-62cm (21½-24½in). In the case of the long-hairs only, the minimum is 54.5cm (21½in) for dogs, 53cm (21in) for bitches.

Below: The Short-haired Hollandse Herder, originally a sheepdog.

Exercise
Needs plenty of exercise to keep in good health.

Grooming
Regular brushing will keep the coat in good condition.

Feeding
Recommended would be 1½-2½ cans (376g, 13.3oz size) of a branded meaty product, with biscuit added in equal part by volume; or 5 cupfuls of a dry food, complete diet, mixed in the proportion of 1 cup of feed to ½ cup of hot or cold water.

Origin and history
The Hollandse Herder is closely related to the Belgian Shepherd Dog and they are of similar origin. It has, however, developed as a separate breed in its native Holland, where it has always been extremely popular.

GERMAN SHEPHERD DOG (Alsatian)

Good points
- *Devoted to owner*
- *Excellent worker/herder*
- *Favoured for obedience trials*
- *Supremely intelligent*
- *Protective*

Take heed
- *Tendency to over-guard*
- *Not a lap dog, but a worker that needs a task in life*

The German Shepherd Dog has one of the largest followings in the world. It is also the breed that rouses the strongest emotions in the public. They either worship the German Shepherd or abhor it. If a smaller breed takes a nip out of the postman's trousers, the misdeed may go unreported; but if a German Shepherd is involved, the headlines are likely to be: 'German Shepherd Dog savages postman!'

The German Shepherd is one of the most courageous and intelligent of dogs, debatably *the* most intelligent. Breed members have fought bravely, and many lost their lives in two World Wars. They have been, and still are, used as guide dogs for the blind (US 'seeing eye dogs'), police dogs, and military dogs. Certainly they are a very popular guard. It is this strong guarding instinct that can be their undoing, however, for a German Shepherd protecting a toddler may menace a stranger at the garden gate. It could also turn nasty through sheer boredom, if acquired as a mere pet dog. The German Shepherd deserves a job to do, whether it be in the public service, or competing eagerly in obedience and working trials.

Below: The German Shepherd Dog, without doubt one of the most intelligent and popular of dogs.

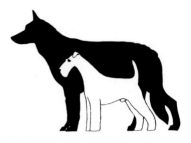

Size
The ideal height (measured to the highest point of the shoulder) is 56-61cm (22-24in) for bitches and 61-66cm (24-26in) for dogs. The proportion of length to height varies between 10:9 and 10:8.5.

Exercise
Needs plenty of exercise, off-the-lead runs and, if possible, obedience exercises. It will excel at the local dog training club in 'scent' and 'retrieve'. Remember that this breed is used to sniff out illegal drug shipments, and to detect the elusive 'black box' amid the wreckage strewn over many miles after airplane crashes.

Grooming
Daily brushing is recommended.

Feeding
Give 1½-2½ cans (376g, 13.3oz size) of a branded meaty product, with biscuit added in equal part by volume; or 5 cupfuls of a dry food, complete diet, mixed in the proportion of 1 cup of food to ½ cup of hot or cold water.

Health care
This is a healthy, hardy breed. However, its popularity in recent years has encouraged indiscriminate breeding, resulting in loss of temperament and form. Take care, when purchasing a German Shepherd Dog, to acquire only from registered HD-free stock. HD is an abbreviation for hip dysplasia, a malformation of the hip joint that can result in the dog being crippled before middle age. Reliable vendors do not breed from affected stock. Many people feel this defect came about through over-emphasis on that desired show dog crouch.

Origin and history
The German Shepherd Dog is attributed by some to the Bronze Age wolf, perhaps an unfortunate suggestion in that it wrongly associates the breed with wolf-like tendencies. Certainly around the 7th century AD a sheepdog of this type, but with a lighter coat, existed in Germany; and by the 16th century the coat had appreciably darkened.

The breed was first exhibited at a dog show in Hanover in 1882. Credit for the formation of the breed is widely assigned to a German fancier named von Stephanitz, who did much to improve its temperament and physical appearance.

The German Shepherd Dog was introduced into Britain following the First World War by a small band of dedicated fanciers who had seen the breed working in Germany. These included the late Colonel Baldwin and Air Commodore Alan Cecil-Wright, President of the Kennel Club. It was thought inappropriate at that time to glorify an animal bearing a German prefix, so, as the breed had come from Alsace, it became known in the United Kingdom as the Alsatian. Only in 1971 did the British Kennel Club relent and agree to the breed being known once more as the German Shepherd Dog. 65▶

DALMATIAN

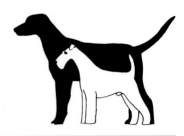

Good points
- *Equable temperament*
- *Loyal*
- *Easy to train*
- *Intelligent*
- *Makes a good house pet*
- *Reliable with children*

Take heed
- *Needs ample exercise*
- *That coat will shed!*

The Dalmatian has a happy nature, is loyal and devoted to its owners and rarely fights. It is easily trained and fairly simple to present in show. It is generally long-lived, and has a lively youth. Remember that it was bred to run with horse and carriage, and has the need and stamina for plenty of exercise.

Size
Overall balance of prime importance, but the ideal height for a dog is 58.5-61cm (23-24in), for a bitch 56-58.5cm (22-23in).

Exercise
Don't buy a Dalmatian unless you can give it plenty of exercise. It is in its element running behind a horse, but an active, open-air country life will suffice.

Grooming
Daily brushing; occasional bathing.

Health care
Some Dalmatians suffer from deafness. Check that a pup can hear before buying.

Feeding
Recommended would be 1½-2½ cans (376g, 13.3oz size) of a branded meaty product, with biscuit added in equal part by volume; or 5 cupfuls of a dry food, complete diet, mixed in the proportion of 1 cup of feed to ½ cup of hot or cold water.

Origin and history
The Dalmatian is often thought of as a British dog, mainly because of its popularity as a carriage dog

Above: Capable of great endurance with a fair amount of speed, the lively Dalmatian will make a loyal companion and thrive as a pet, provided it is given plenty of exercise in open countryside.

in the 18th century, but in fact it originated in Yugoslavia. The breed has enjoyed an upsurge in popularity since 1959, when Walt Disney made a film of Dodie Smith's enchanting book, *A Hundred and One Dalmatians*. It is still shown on the cinema circuits during children's holiday periods, and has a healthy effect on Dalmatian registrations. Mrs E.J. Woodyatt's Champion Fanhill Faune won Best in Show at Crufts in February 1978. 66▶

Shar-Pei 14▶

Bulldog 16▶

Elkhound 22▶

Samoyed 18▶

Siberian
Husky 17▶

Standard
Poodle 19▶

Irish Water
Spaniel 21▶

American Water Spaniel 21 ▶

Karelian
Bear Dog 24▶

Swedish
Elkhound 23▶

Beauceron
25▶

English
Springer
Spaniel 20▶

Clumber
Spaniel 26▶

Smalands Hound 31▶

Hygen
Hound 33▶

Schiller
Hound 32▶

Finnish
Hound 32▶

Halden
Hound 33▶

English
Foxhound 29▶

Dunker Hound 31▶

American
Foxhound 30▶

Harrier 27▶

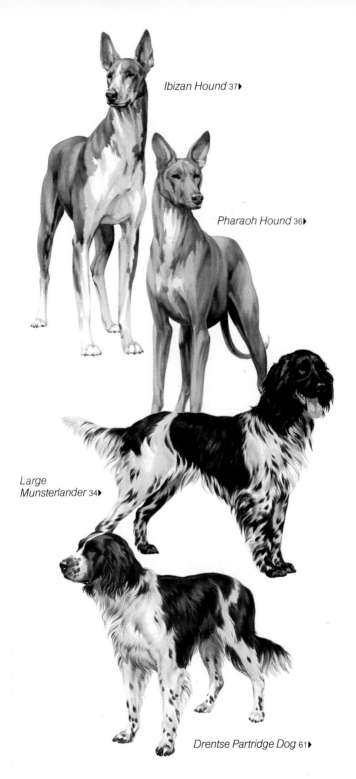

Ibizan Hound 37▶

Pharaoh Hound 36▶

Large
Munsterlander 34▶

Drentse Partridge Dog 61▶

61

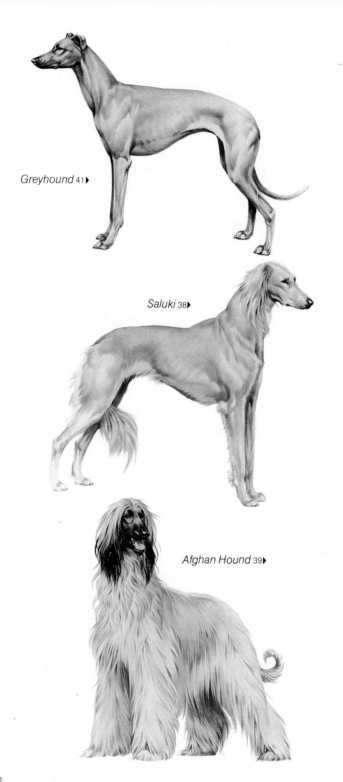

Greyhound 41▶

Saluki 38▶

Afghan Hound 39▶

Airedale 42▶

Dobermann 43▶

Bearded
Collie 45▶

Smooth Collie 46▶

Rough Collie 46▶

63

German
Short-haired
Pointer 47▶

Pointer 48▶

Irish Setter 49▶

English
Setter 50▶

Gordon
Setter 51▶

German Shepherd Dog 54▶

*Belgian
Shepherd Dog
(Groenendael)* 52▶

Golden Retriever 78▶

*Labrador
Retriever* 79▶

Weimaraner 75▶

Dalmatian 56▶

Boxer 76▶

Belgian
Shepherd Dog
(Malinois) 52▶

Belgian Shepherd Dog
(Laekenois) 52▶

Belgian
Shepherd Dog
(Tervueren) 52▶

Curly-coated Retriever 82▶

Chesapeake Bay Retriever 81▶

Flat-coated Retriever 80▶

Eskimo Dog 88▶

Alaskan Malamute 87▶

67

Otterhound 89▶

Italian Spinone 90▶

Japanese Akita 86▶

Chow Chow 68▶

Bouvier des Flandres 94▶

Briard 95▶

Rottweiler 91▶

*Rhodesian
Ridgeback* 84▶

Hungarian Vizsla 44▶

Hungarian Kuvasz 98▶

Great Swiss Mountain Dog 99▶

Bernese Mountain Dog 99▶

70

Borzoi 104▶

*Anatolian
Shepherd Dog* 101▶

*Black and Tan
Coonhound* 96▶

Bloodhound 97▶

*Estrela
Mountain Dog* 100▶

Tibetan Mastiff 103▶

71

Irish
Wolfhound 106▶

Deerhound 105▶

Polish Sheepdog
(Lowlands) 92▶

Old English
Sheepdog 93▶

Leonberger 107▶

*Pyrenean
Mountain Dog* 108▶

Komondor 110▶

*Maremma
Sheepdog* 109▶

73

Bullmastiff 111▶

Neopolitan Mastiff 112▶

Mastiff 113▶

Great Dane 115▶

Giant
Schnauzer 114▶

St Bernard 116▶

Newfoundland 117▶

WEIMARANER

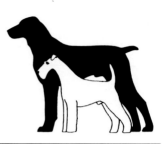

Good points
- *Distinctive appearance*
- *Does not shed*
- *Excels in obedience competitions*
- *Fine gundog*
- *Good temperament*

Take heed
- *Likes to have a job of work to do*
- *Thrives best if kept indoors*

The Weimaraner (or Silver Ghost) is an excellent gundog, which originally hunted big game. It is obedient and eminently trainable, excelling in obedience competitions, and has been used as both police dog and guard. It makes a good pet, but is happiest when given a job to do.

Size
Height at withers: dog 61-68.5cm (24-27in), bitch 56-63.5cm (22-25in).

Exercise
Needs plenty; has boundless energy. No need to rule out town living, but it is essential that the Weimaraner has lots of supervised freedom.

Grooming
Needs very little brushing, if any, for its sleek coat will naturally free itself of mud. Clip nails when necessary.

Feeding
Recommended would be 1½-2½ cans (376g, 13.3oz size) of a branded meaty product, with biscuit added in equal part by volume; or 5 cupfuls of a dry food, complete diet, mixed in the proportion of 1 cup of feed to ½ cup of hot or cold water.

Origin and history.
The Weimaraner burst upon the British scene in the early 1950s, since when it has become popular as a family pet, show dog and contender in obedience competitions. It is also well thought of in the United States, the best stock being available in those two countries. But the Weimaraner is in fact no newcomer, having been purpose-bred as a gundog at the court in Weimar, Germany, towards the end of the 18th century. Bloodhounds, Pointers and the old St Hubert Hounds are said to have assisted in its make-up. Its silver-grey colour is extremely distinctive. 66▶

Below: With its distinctive pale eyes and metallic silver-grey coat, the Weimaraner is as striking in appearance as it is impressive as a first-rate gundog.

BOXER

Good points
- *Brave*
- *Clownish*
- *Good guard*
- *Loves children*
- *Loyal*
- *Impressive show dog*

Take heed
- *Enjoys a scrap and respects opponents smaller than itself!*

The Boxer is a delightful animal that takes longer than most to grow up. It loves children and is a faithful protector of the family. However, it is an exuberant, fairly powerful dog, deserving a reasonable-sized home and garden and owners prepared to spend the necessary time on exercising and training. It has served in the armed forces and as a guide dog for the blind (seeing eye dog). Its tail is docked, and when pleased it tends to wag its whole body with pleasure.

Size
Height at the withers: dog 56-61cm (22-24in); bitch 53-58.5cm (21-23in). Weight: dogs around 58.5cm (23in) should weigh about 30kg (66lb); and bitches of about 56cm (22in) should weigh about 28.1kg (62lb).

Exercise
Good daily walks and off-the-lead runs are recommended.

Grooming
Daily brushing is sufficient.

Feeding
Recommended would be 1½-2½ cans (376g, 13.3oz size) of a branded meaty product, with biscuit added in equal part by volume; or 5 cupfuls of a dry food, complete diet, mixed in the proportion of 1 cup of feed to ½ cup of hot or cold water.

Origin and history
The Boxer is traceable to the old holding dogs of Mollossus or Mastiff type, which the Cimbrians took into battle against the Romans. Like the Bulldog, its jaw is undershot, a trait common in bull-baiters. The Brabant bull-baiter, from which the English Bulldog evolved, also played its part in the evolution of the Boxer, which retains its fighting spirit to this day. 66▶

Below: The Boxer is renowned for its enthusiasm and lively personality.

CHOW CHOW

Good points
- *Beautiful*
- *Loyal*
- *Odour-free*

Take heed
- *Formidable opponent*
- *Needs firm gentle handling*
- *Strong willed*
- *One-man dog (but will accept owner's family)*

The Chow Chow, whose name is perhaps derived from the Chinese Choo Hunting Dog, is a member of the Spitz family known for over 2000 years, lion-like in appearance and famed for its black tongue. It is odour-free and makes an incredibly loyal companion, tending to devote itself to one member of the family though accepting and returning the affection of other household members. It needs quiet but firm handling: with its aloof temperament it is unlikely to deign to walk at your heel without persuasion. It does not take kindly to strangers and is a fearsome fighter if provoked.

The Chow Chow is an extremely successful show dog; its beautiful coat and dignified appearance attract great attention from visitors and fellow competitors.

Size
Minimum height for Chows is 46cm (18in), but in every case balance should be the outstanding feature and height left to the discretion of the judges.

Exercise
Most Chow owners seem to manage with regular on-the-lead walks with runs in permitted areas. However, mindful of the Chow's prowess as a hunter of wolves, game and anything that moves, it seems unfair to keep it in confined surroundings or to deprive it of the open spaces that it relishes.

Grooming
About 5 or 10 minutes' brushing a day and about an hour each weekend with a wire brush should keep the Chow gleaming.

Feeding
One to 1½ cans (376g, 13.3oz size) of a branded meaty product, with biscuit added in equal part by volume; or 3 cupfuls of dry, complete food mixed in the proportion of 1 cup of feed to ½ cup of hot or cold water. Perhaps not surprisingly, they also do well on rice or on tripe, chicken and lean beef.

Origin and history
Although there are other black-mouthed dogs, the Chow is the only dog with a black tongue, although small bears — to which it has some resemblance — share this characteristic. Reputed to be the original Lama's Mastiff, the Chow Chow must be one of the oldest members of the Spitz family and was bred variously for its flesh — which in many parts of Asia is considered a delicacy — and for its fur and as a useful hunter of game. In early Chinese writings, it was known as the Tartar Dog, or Dog of Barbarians. The first breed members imported into England, in 1760, were exhibited in a zoo. Sadly, a reputation for ferocity has come down with the Chow, yet it is an affectionate, devoted animal. It is unlikely to fight unless provoked, but then it will be a formidable opponent. The Chow Chow Club was formed in England in 1895 and today around 600 or 700 breed members a year are registered with the British Kennel Club, and interest in the breed is constantly growing. 68▶

GOLDEN RETRIEVER

Good points
- *Excellent gundog*
- *Gentle with children*
- *Sound temperament*
- *Intelligent*
- *Easy to train*
- *First-class show dog*
- *Good family pet*

Take heed
- *No drawbacks known*

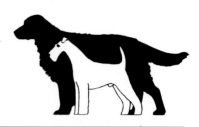

The Golden Retriever cannot be too highly recommended as a breed to suit all the family. It will romp with the children, enjoy a day's shooting with the man of the house, and happily accompany the mistress on a shopping trip, or for a session at the dog training club. This is a trustworthy breed, which can be kennelled, but individuals are happiest sharing the fireside with their family. They love to retrieve and will enjoy nothing better than carrying the newspaper home, or wandering around the house with an old chewed slipper. They are often used as guide dogs (seeing eye dogs) for the blind.

Size
The average weight in good hard condition should be: dog 31.8-36.3kg (70-80lb); bitch 27.2-31.8kg (60-70lb). Height at shoulder: dog 56-61cm (22-24in); bitch 51-56cm (20-22in).

Exercise
Needs at least an hour's exercise every day, and free runs, also an ample garden.

Grooming
Regular brushing will keep the coat in good condition.

Feeding
Recommended would be 1½-2½ cans (376g, 13.3oz size) of a branded meaty product, with biscuit added in equal part by volume; or 5 cupfuls of a dry food, complete diet, mixed in the proportion of 1 cup of feed to ½ cup of hot or cold water.

Origin and history
There is some controversy as to the origin of this breed. Did it, as many like to believe, develop from a troupe of Russian shepherd dogs found by Lord Tweedmouth performing in a Brighton circus in 1860, or did it begin with a litter of golden-haired pups of retriever/spaniel ancestry born on his Scottish estate? Romanticists like to believe the tale that Lord Tweedmouth was so greatly impressed with the Russian shepherd dogs that he bought the entire troupe and bred from them, adding Bloodhound blood to develop the nose. It is a theory that still has enthusiasts arguing. 65▶

Below: The Golden Retriever is second to none as a gentle and trustworthy pet for all the family.

LABRADOR RETRIEVER

Good points
- *Equable temperament*
- *Excellent gundog*
- *Good family pet*
- *Kind with children*
- *Easy to train*
- *Intelligent*
- *First-class showdog*

Take heed
- *No drawbacks known*

Like the Golden Retriever, the Labrador Retriever cannot be too highly recommended as a breed tailor-made to suit the whole family. It is an excellent retriever, can be trusted with the children and will give a good account of itself in obedience training competitions. The Labrador Retriever is a breed much favoured as a guide dog (seeing eye dog) for the blind.

Size
Height: dog 56-57cm (22-22½in); bitch 54.5-56cm (21½-22in).

Exercise
Needs an hour a day at least, with free runs, also an ample garden.

Grooming
Regular brushing will keep the coat in good condition.

Feeding
Recommended would be 1½-2½ cans (376g, 13.3oz size) of a branded meaty product, with biscuit added in equal part by volume; or 5 cupfuls of a dry food, complete diet, mixed in the proportion of 1 cup of feed to ½ cup of water.

Origin and history
The Labrador Retriever came to Britain with fishermen from Newfoundland (not Labrador) in the 1830s, the dog's task in those days being to land the nets of the fishermen; their ability to swim has survived. Among the most popular British gundogs, they are also much sought after as family pets in many parts of the world. 65▶

Below: The Labrador Retriever makes a gentle, intelligent pet.

FLAT-COATED RETRIEVER

Good points
- *Can live kennelled or as a housepet*
- *Easy to train*
- *Good with children*
- *Hardy*
- *Natural retriever*
- *Good guard dog*

Take heed
- *No drawbacks known*

The Flat-coated Retriever is likely to enjoy renewed popularity since attaining the coveted Best in Show award at Crufts in 1980. It is a natural retriever, used for picking up game; it is hardy and easily trained, and makes a good household companion if you wish, being very good with children.

Size
Should be 27.2-31.8kg (60-70lb).

Exercise
Thrives on plenty of exercise.

Grooming
Regular brushing and tidying up.

Feeding
Recommended would be 1½-2½ cans (376g, 13.3oz size) of a branded meaty product, with biscuit added in equal part by volume; or 5 cupfuls of a dry food,

complete diet, mixed in the proportion of 1 cup of feed to ½ cup of hot or cold water.

Origin and history
The Flat-coat probably owes its evolution to the Labrador Retriever, the Collie and certain spaniels. It was at one time known as the Wavy-coated Retriever, and it is thought that Collie blood was introduced to produce the Flat-coat. Prior to the First World War the Flat-coat was perhaps the best-known gundog in Britain, but it was over-shadowed in the post-war era by the Golden Retriever and Labrador Retriever, whose appeal has remained constant, not, however, to the detriment of the quality of the Flat-coat breed. 67▶

Below: The Flat-coated Retriever is a strongly-built working dog that will make a dependable pet.

CHESAPEAKE BAY RETRIEVER

Good points
- *First-class retriever*
- *Sportsman's favourite*
- *Usually good with children*
- *Intelligent*
- *Devoted to owner*

Take heed
- *Occasionally aggressive*
- *Oily coat may be off-putting to some people*

The Chesapeake Bay is a favourite with American sportsmen but has to date few devotees in the United Kingdom. It is an excellent swimmer and an unsurpassed retriever of wild duck. It is generally good with children, but can be a little headstrong and difficult to train. Distinguishing features are the breed's yellow eyes and web feet. Its coat is water-resistant.

Size
Weight: dog 29.5-34kg (65-75lb), bitch 25-29.5kg (55-65lb). Height: dog 58.5-66cm (23-26in), bitch 53-61cm (21-24in).

Exercise
Needs plenty of hard exercise to stay in good condition.

Grooming
Normal brushing is sufficient.

Feeding
Recommended would be 1½-2½ cans (376g, 13.3oz size) of a branded meaty product, with biscuit added in equal part by volume; or 5 cupfuls of a dry food, complete diet, mixed in the proportion of 1 cup of feed to ½ cup of hot or cold water.

Origin and history
This is an American retriever of British origin. An English brig went aground off the coast of Maryland in 1807 and was rescued by an American ship, the *Canton*. Aboard the brig were two pups, which were named 'Canton', after the rescue ship, and 'Sailor'. They were subsequently trained to

Above: Not widely kept as a household pet, the Chesapeake Bay Retriever has many admirers for its abilities as a sporting dog. Its web feet and oily, water-resistant coat make it well suited for retrieving wild duck.

retrieve duck, and crossed with Otterhounds and the Curly-coated and Flat-coated Retriever. The pups are said to have been Newfoundland in origin. Americans seem to want to retain the breed as a sporting dog, which is why it has not found its way into many homes as a pet. People either rave about the merits of the Chesapeake Bay, or are completely put off by their oily coats, not unpleasant oily odour, and yellow-orange eyes. 67▶

CURLY-COATED RETRIEVER

Good points
- *Beautiful appearance*
- *Equable temperament*
- *Excellent guard*
- *Fine swimmer*
- *Good nose/retriever*
- *Full of stamina*
- *Intelligent*

Take heed
- *No drawbacks known*

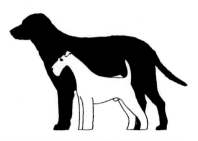

The Curly-coat is an excellent worker on land and in water, and will retrieve any game. It is a hardy dog, of good temperament and fine appearance. One wonders why its numbers have diminished.

Size
Weight: 31.8-36.3kg (70-80lb).
Height: 63.5-68.5cm (25-27in).

Exercise
Thrives on liberal amounts of vigorous exercise.

Grooming
Don't brush and comb this breed Just damp the coat down and massage with circular movements. Seek advice on trimming.

Feeding
Recommended would be 1½-2½ cans (376g, 13.3oz size) of a branded meaty product, with biscuit added in equal part by volume; or 5 cupfuls of a dry food, complete diet, mixed in the proportion of 1 cup of feed to ½ cup of hot or cold water.

Origin and history
The Curly-coat was one of the earliest British retrievers. It was exhibited at dog shows in England as early as 1860 and was depicted in many sporting prints beforehand. Its popularity seems to have waned since the beginning of the First World War and, despite its superb working ability, it has never been in great demand since. The early Labrador obviously played a part in its make-up and, to hazard a suggestion, the Water Spaniel, which, with its tight curly coat, it closely resembles. 67▶

Below: Bred for retrieving game from thick cover and water, the Curly-coated Retriever makes a faithful companion and house pet.

HOVAWART

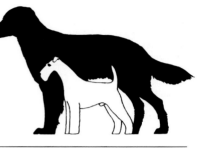

Good points
- *Excellent guard*
- *Home-loving*
- *Fond of children*
- *Loyal*
- *Obedient*

Take heed
- *Slow to mature*
- *Tends to be a one-person dog*
- *Will fight if challenged*

The Hovawart is an old German breed which, like so many of similar origin, was not bred for a specific purpose. It is, and always has been, just a loyal companion dog and protector of the home. The German Kennel Club recognized the breed in 1936.

It is generally obedient, loves children, and has utter loyalty to its master, tending to be a one-person dog, although defending the entire family with its life. It is good natured, but will fight well if put to the test.

Size
Height: 63.5-68.5cm (25-27in); Weight: 29.5-40.8kg (65-90lb): bitches less.

Exercise
Normal regular exercise.

Grooming
Regular brushing will keep the coat shining and in good condition.

Feeding
Recommended would be 1½-2½ cans (376g, 13.3oz size) of a branded meaty product, with biscuit added in equal part by volume; or 5 cupfuls of a dry food, complete diet, mixed as 1 cup of feed to ½ cup of hot or cold water.

Origin and history
The Hovawart was already a popular companion dog in Germany during the Middle Ages. In fact, the name Hovawart means 'house guard'. It resembles the Kuvasz in stature and looks like a large Collie. The breed seems to have suffered a period of unpopularity, but after the First World War such specimens as could be found were crossed with Leonbergers and Newfoundlands to perpetuate a once famous breed.

Below: The loyal Hovawart will instinctively defend its owners.

RHODESIAN RIDGEBACK

Good points
- *Affectionate*
- *Obedient*
- *Good with children*
- *Superior intelligence*
- *Sense of fun*

Take heed
- *Will guard you, and your possessions, with its life!*
- *Deserves a large garden*

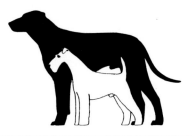

The Rhodesian Ridgeback is a handsome, muscular, medium-sized dog of the hound group, with a short tan-coloured coat, pendulous ears and a long, uncropped tail.

The breed is named after the line of hair, shaped like the blade of a broadsword, that grows in the reverse direction along the back, with two crowns at the shoulder and the point towards the tail. This ridge is a very distinctive marking that is not found in any other breed of dog.

Although the ridge may appear to be a superficiality, created for the show ring or as a talking point, in fact it is far from recent and has come down through the centuries by way of the African Hottentot Hunting Dog.

The Rhodesian Ridgeback is of a quiet temperament and rarely barks; it enjoys spending hours curled up lazily in the corner of a room, stretched out in the summer sun, or basking in front of an open fireplace. Although its exploits as a hunter of African game first brought it recognition, the breed was developed as a dual-purpose dog, as a hunter and a gentle guardian of the families of the early white settlers. More and more people are discovering the tranquil temperament of this breed, its affectionate disposition and desire for human companionship. The Ridgeback likes nothing better than to lean against you, or to sit on your feet. And if you own a diamond, this is just the dog to guard it!

Below: A beautiful Rhodesian Ridgeback with her unweaned puppies.

Size
The desirable weight is: dog 36.3kg (80lb), bitch 31.75kg (70lb), with a permissible variation of 2.3kg (5lb) above and below these weights. A mature Ridgeback should be a handsome, upstanding animal; dogs should be of a height of 63.5-68.5cm (25-27in) and bitches 61-66cm (24-26in). Minimum bench standard: dog 63.5cm (25in), bitch 61cm (24in).

Exercise
This large, sleepy and apparently slow-moving animal with its characteristic love of lazing, contrasts sharply with its action when alerted. In a flash, it is converted into a graceful streak of rhythmic motion, a pleasure to watch as it quickly overtakes a rabbit or a squirrel in full flight. This is a pet that should have a large garden to run in, and deserves a master able to give it a good walk every day.

Grooming
Daily grooming with a hound glove, coupled with correct feeding and plenty of exercise, will keep the Ridgeback in healthy and gleaming condition.

Feeding
About 1½-2½ cans of branded dog food (376g, 13.3oz size), supplemented by biscuit, should be sufficient for your Ridgeback. Or, if you prefer, 5 cupfuls of a dry food, complete diet, mixed in the proportion of 1 cup of feed to ½ cup of hot or cold water. And of course, like most breeds, the Ridgeback will enjoy meat scraps and the occasional large bone.

Remember that suggested quantities are only a guide, and should be increased or decreased according to the desired weight of your dog. Watch it carefully, and if it appears to be putting on undue weight, cut down on the biscuit.

Origin and history
Long before Europeans settled in South Africa, the members of the Hottentot tribe had, as a companion who accompanied them on their hunting expeditions, an animal that has since been called the Hottentot Hunting Dog, a distinct characteristic of which was the ridge of hair growing in the reverse direction along its back.

During the 16th and 17th centuries, Dutch, Boers, Germans and Huguenots migrated to South Africa and, as these people were pioneers in a new and uncivilized country teeming with fierce wild animals, they brought with them their own European medium-sized and large working and hunting dogs. Probably by chance, the white settlers' dogs became crossed with the tough Hottentot Hunting Dogs, and the superior quality and vigour of their offspring were quickly recognized, the presence of the ridge identifying the most desirable dogs.

This blending over 200 years of the best qualities of many European breeds with those of the Hottentot Hunting Dog formed the immediate ancestor of today's Ridgeback, which has many of the characteristics usually associated with other hounds. 69▶

JAPANESE AKITA (Akita)

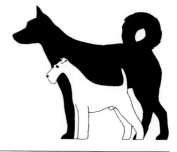

Good points
- Strong and courageous
- Easily trained
- First-class guard
- Versatile hunter/retriever
- Good temperament
- Intelligent
- Extremely faithful

Take heed
- Needs firm but gentle discipline

The Japanese Akita is the best-known of the Japanese Spitz breeds but has only recently come on the international scene. The breed has been exhibited in recent years in the United Kingdom and America, and the Japanese are doing all possible to improve their purebred stock. Bred as a hunter of wild boar, deer and even black bear, the Akita is undoubtedly capable of ferocity, but it is easily trained and generally has an equable temperament.

Size
Height: dog 53-61cm (21-24in), some bigger; bitch 48-53cm (19-21in). Weight: 38.6-49.9kg (85-110lb).

Exercise
Does not require a great deal of exercise. Incidentally, it has webbed feet and is a fine swimmer and a good water dog.

Grooming
Normal daily brushing.

Feeding
Recommended would be 1½-2½ cans (376g, 13.3oz size) of a branded meaty product, with biscuit added in equal part by volume; or 5 cupfuls of a dry food, complete diet, mixed in the proportion of 1 cup of feed to ½ cup of hot or cold water.

Origin and history
The Akita resembles a smooth-coated Chow and is the largest of the known Japanese Spitz breeds. It is bred in its native land as a

Above: The Japanese Akita is highly respected for its fearless spirit.

hunter of wild boar and deer, and is obviously related to the Icelandic breeds. However, it has bred true in Japan's Akita Province for more than 300 years, and its exact origin is obscure.

The Akita is revered in Japan for its hunting and retrieving skills, particularly its stamina for working in deep snow and its ability to retrieve waterfowl and even drive fish into fishermen's nets. In 1931 the breed was officially appointed a national treasure and monument of Japan.

American servicemen returning after the Second World War took the Akita home and boosted its popularity in America. 68▶

ALASKAN MALAMUTE

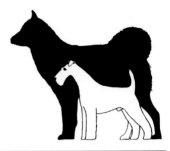

Good points
- *Affectionate*
- *Fast and strong*
- *Fine sled dog*
- *Loves children*
- *Intelligent*
- *Sociable*

Take heed
- *Needs firm but gentle discipline and vigorous exercise*

The Alaskan Malamute is an Arctic Spitz-type little known outside Alaska and the United States. It is a sociable dog, capable of being driven in sled races by children. It is highly prized as a sled dog, and capable of immense speed. Don't be put off by the wolfish appearance: the kindly expression is genuine!

Size
Height: dog 63.5-71cm (25-28in); bitch 58.5-66cm (23-26in). Weight: 38.6-56.7kg (85-125lb).

Exercise
Needs plenty of vigorous exercise to stay healthy.

Grooming
Regular brushing will keep the coat in good condition.

Feeding
Recommended would be 1½-2½ cans (376g, 13.3oz size) of a branded meaty product, with biscuit added in equal part by volume; or 5 cupfuls of a dry food, complete diet, mixed in the proportion of 1 cup of feed to ½ cup of hot or cold water.

Origin and history
The Alaskan Malamute is named after a native tribe called the Mahlemuts. The origin of the dogs is obscure, but the breed is obviously closely related to other Spitz-types, such as the Samoyed. 67▶

Below: The Alaskan Malamute combines great strength, stamina and beauty in the shape of a fine working dog and an affectionate companion.

ESKIMO DOG /GREENLAND DOG

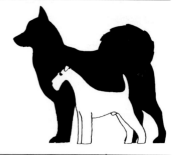

Good points
- *Beautiful appearance*
- *Can become devoted*
- *Great endurance*
- *Excellent sled dogs*
- *Strong*
- *Fine guards*

Take heed
- *Rarely live indoors*
- *Suspicious of strangers*

The Eskimo Dog is one of several regional sled dogs of different names, few of which are well known outside the polar area. It is hardy, and accustomed to fending for itself, living outside and often having to find its own food.

The Greenland Dog is so similar that controversy rages as to whether they shoud be separately classified. There is also an Icelandic Sheepdog which is similar in appearance to the Finnish Spitz and Norwegian Buhund.

Size
Height at shoulder: dog 58.5-68.5cm (23-27in); bitch 51-61cm (20-24in). Weight: dog 34-47.6kg (75-105lb); bitch 27.2-40.8kg (60-90lb).

Exercise
These dogs are accustomed to pulling sleds and hauling fishing boats ashore. They would soon get bored snoozing by the fire.

Grooming
Regular brushing will keep the coat in good condition.

Feeding
Recommended would be 1½-2½ cans (376g. 13.3oz size) of a branded meaty product, with biscuit added in equal part by volume; or 5 cupfuls of a dry food, complete diet, mixed in the proportion of 1 cup of feed to ½ cup of hot or cold water.

Origin and history
These polar Spitz breeds no doubt originated in Eastern Siberia and shared a common task and ancestry with the Alaskan Malamute, Siberian Husky and Samoyed. To quote the American explorer Peary, 'there is, in fact, only one sled dog'. 67▶

Below: The rugged and good-natured Eskimo dog may not adapt well to domestic life as a house pet.

OTTERHOUND

Good points
- Appealing
- Excellent swimmer
- Friendly
- Gentle with children
- Waterproof coat

Take heed
- Essentially a hound rather than a house pet, and not ideally suited to suburban living

With otter hunting now outlawed in the United Kingdom, the Otterhound could have faced extinction, had not the last Master of the Kendal and District Otterhounds, in the Lake District, set up the Otterhound Club to ensure the survival of the breed. Without the continued interest of breeders and the show world, the Otterhound would certainly die out.

The Otterhound is an amiable, friendly animal, gentle with children and responsive to affection. However, one should not lose sight of the fact that it was a pack hound bred to kill, a background that does not ideally equip it as a household pet.

Size
Height: dogs should stand approximately 68.5cm (27in) at the shoulder; bitches approximately 61cm (24in). Weight: dogs 34-52.2kg (75-115lb); bitches 29.5-45.4kg (65-100lb).

Exercise
The Otterhound needs a lot of exercise. A unique feature of this breed is the existence of webbing between the toes. This gives the Otterhound a decided advantage in the water. Most dogs can swim, but the Otterhound excels in that ability, and is as much at home in the water as it is on land.

Grooming
A thorough brush and comb once a week should be sufficient to keep the Otterhound's coat in good condition. There is natural oil in the coat and, if bathing the animal for a

show, it is advisable to do this a week beforehand to allow the coat to regain its correct texture. However, the head hair can be bathed the day before a show because this is of a finer texture.

Particular attention must be paid to the ears, as they are inclined to collect wax and can become a source of irritation to the animal. Inspect the ears regularly.

Feeding
The Otterhound is a large dog and will need up to 2½ cans of a good branded meaty diet (376g, 13.3oz size) to which biscuit should be added in equal part by volume; or 5 cupfuls of a dry food, complete diet, mixed in the proportion of 1 cup of feed to ½ cup of hot or cold water.

Origin and history
The Otterhound is an extremely old breed, and its origins are somewhat obscure. Some say it descended from the old Southern Hound and others see the Bloodhound in its ancestry. Today it is most like some of the French hounds, such as the Griffon Nivernais or Griffon Vendéen, and it is quite possible that the Otterhound springs from the same origins as these French breeds.

Otter hunting was one of the earliest field sports in the United Kingdom and King John, Henry II and Elizabeth I all kept Otterhound packs, long before foxes were thought worthy to be hunted. Many monasteries also kept Otterhounds to protect their fishponds from the nightly ravages of otters. 68▶

ITALIAN SPINONE

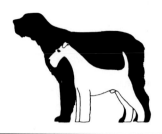

Good points
- *Affectionate*
- *Fine retriever of water fowl*
- *Hardy*
- *Good guard dog*
- *Easy to train*
- *Loyal companion*

Take heed
- *No drawbacks known*

The Italian Spinone is an ancient breed of gundog, much appreciated by Italian horsemen for its ability to work in marshy and wooded country. It has a soft mouth and will point and retrieve. It is good-natured and well established in its own country.

Size
Height: dog 60-65cm (23½-25½in); bitch 54.5-60cm (21½-23½in).

Exercise
Needs plenty of vigorous exercise.

Grooming
Daily brushing will be sufficient.

Feeding
Recommended would be 1½-2½ cans (376g, 13.3oz size) of a branded meaty product, with biscuit added in equal part by volume; or 5 cupfuls of a dry food, complete diet, mixed in the proportion of 1 cup of feed to ½ cup of hot or cold water.

Origin and history
The Spinone originated in the French region of Bresse but later found its way to Piedmont in Italy, its evolution being attributable to the French Griffon, French and German Pointers, the Porçelaine, Barbet and Korthals Griffon. What has emerged is a reliable gundog with a pleasing appearance, somewhere between a Pointer and a Foxhound. 68▶

Below: The friendly and rugged Italian Spinone is a popular gundog and show dog in its native country.

ROTTWEILER

Good points
- *Good temperament*
- *Intelligent*
- *Makes a good household companion/guard*
- *Reliable working dog*

Take heed
- *Responds best to kind, firm handling — not being chained or kennelled in a back yard*

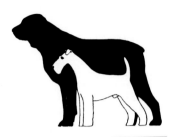

The Rottweiler is a German working dog of high intelligence and good temperament. It has been a draught dog and herder, and is still used as guard, police dog, sled dog and mountain rescue dog. In many countries it is sought after as a companion/pet and guard. It is a popular contender in the show ring and does well in obedience tests.

Size
Height at shoulder: dog 63.5-68.5cm (25-27in); bitch 58.5-63.5cm (23-25in).

Exercise
Regular walks and runs.

Grooming
Daily brushing will keep the coat in good condition.

Feeding
Recommended would be 1½-2½ cans (376g, 13.3oz size) of a branded meaty product, with biscuit added in equal part by volume; or 5 cupfuls of a dry food, complete diet, mixed in the proportion of 1 cup of feed to ½ cup of hot or cold water.

Origin and history
The Rottweiler is a butcher's dog. It comes from the West German town of Rottweil in Württemberg, where it is known as the Rottweiler Metzgerhund or Rottweil butcher's dog.

It was known in the Middle Ages as a hunter of wild boar, and later as a revered and trusted cattle dog as well as a draught dog that would draw carts for butchers and cattle dealers. Just before the first World War its abilities were recognized as a police dog and guard.

Thelma Gray of the Rozavel Kennels introduced the breed into Britain in 1936. It was developing a following until World War II, when breeding ceased, and it was not until a Captain Roy-Smith, serving with the Occupation Army in Germany, brought home a dog and bitch that a sound breeding programme was re-established, since when a few breed devotees have produced many good specimens. 69▶

Below: Excellent as a guard and police dog, the powerful Rottweiler will also make a reliable and affectionate companion for the family.

POLISH SHEEPDOG (Owczarek Podhalanski, Owczarek Nizinny)

Good points
- *Excellent guard*
- *Hardy*
- *Generally good-natured*
- *Intelligent*

Take heed
- *No drawbacks known. However, the Nizinny is generally thought to be the more docile of the two varieties*

Lowlands type

There are two varieties of Polish Sheepdog, the Lowlands Shepherd Dog (Owczarek Nizinny), which looks something like the Old English Sheepdog, and the Tatry Mountain Sheepdog (Owczarek Podhalanski), a bigger type that has something of the Retriever or Kuvasz about its appearance. They are both intelligent, good-natured, generally docile and have a keen memory.

Size
Height: Tatry Mountain Sheepdog 66cm (26in); Lowlands Shepherd Dog 40.5-51cm (16-20in).

Exercise
Plenty of exercise necessary.

Below: The Lowlands Shepherd Dog, a hardy sheepdog from Poland.

Grooming
Regular brushing; the Lowlands type will need combing with a steel comb also.

Feeding
Recommended would be 1½-2½ cans (376g, 13.3oz size) of a branded meaty product, with biscuit added in equal part by volume; or 5 cupfuls of a dry food, complete diet, mixed in the proportion of 1 cup of feed to ½ cup of hot or cold water.

Origin and history
The Tatry Mountain Sheepdog bears a strong similarity to the Hungarian Kuvasz, and both varieties are credited with having been introduced to Poland in the 4th or 5th century. They are little known outside their homeland. 72▶

OLD ENGLISH SHEEPDOG

Good points
- *Beautiful appearance*
- *Home-loving*
- *Intelligent*
- *Adaptable to different climates*
- *Excellent with children*
- *Gets on well with other animals*
- *Sound temperament*

Take heed
- *Not suitable for confined quarters*

The Old English Sheepdog, or Bobtail, is an extremely popular breed, being a devoted friend and guardian of children, with a sound, sensible temperament. It will live contentedly in a fairly small house despite its bulk.

Size
Height: dog 56cm (22in) and upwards; bitch slightly less.

Exercise
Regular walks of average length — perhaps two good walks of 20 minutes duration per day.

Grooming
Daily brushing and weekly combing with a steel comb. The hair is

Below: The ever-popular Old English Sheepdog, a playful and devoted pet.

brushed forward to cover the eyes. I don't know how, but it *can* see! White parts are powdered for showing.

Health care
Check the ears for canker, and take care that dead, matted hair does not accumulate around the feet. Some Bobtails are born with that stumpy tail; otherwise it is docked to a length of 5cm (2in).

Feeding
Recommended would be 1½-2½ cans (376g, 13.3oz size) of a branded meaty product, with biscuit added in equal part by volume; or 5 cupfuls of a dry food, complete diet, mixed in the proportion of 1 cup of feed to ½ cup of hot or cold water.

Origin and history
The Old English Sheepdog is often, for obvious reasons, known as the Bobtail. How it came to England is a subject of conjecture, for the breed is said to have evolved through the crossing of the Briard with the large Russian Owtscharka, a dog related to the Hungarian sheep-dogs. It was used in England as a cattle dog and guard, but nowadays is kept mainly as a much loved pet. Because of the Bobtail's reliability with children, a number have found their way into schools for handicapped young-sters. The first breed club for the Old English Sheepdog was estab-lished in Britain in 1888 and the standard has altered little in the intervening years. 72▶

BOUVIER DES FLANDRES

Good points
- *Strong and alert*
- *Easily trained*
- *Impressive guard*
- *Loyal to owner's family*
- *Trustworthy*

Take heed
- *Fierce appearance, especially with cropped ears*
- *One-person family dog*

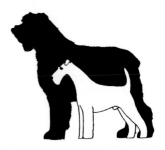

The Bouvier des Flandres is a Belgian cattle dog, hardy, trustworthy, and — when its ears are cropped, as in its country of origin — looking the epitome of ferocity. It can be kept as a pet, but tends to be a one-person dog, though that means guarding their family as well!

Size
Weight: dog 34.9-39.9kg (77-88lb); bitch 27-34.9kg (59½-77lb). Height: dog 62-68.5cm (24½-27in); bitch 58.5-65cm (23-25½in).

Exercise
Needs plenty of exercise. Not ideally suited to town life.

Grooming
Regular brushing will keep the coat in good condition.

Feeding
Recommended would be 1½-2½ cans (376g, 13.3oz size) of a branded meaty product, with biscuit added in equal part by volume; or 5 cupfuls of a dry food, complete diet, mixed in the proportion of 1 cup of feed to ½ cup of hot or cold water.

Origin and history
The Bouvier was derived from a number of working Belgian breeds with the purpose of producing a good all-purpose dog, suitable for the rough shoot, for herding, and also as a draught dog. It was not until 1912 that a meeting was held to discuss a possible standard for the Bouvier; no agreement was reached, and devotees had to wait until after the First World War for a standard to be drawn up by the Club National Belge du Bouvier des Flandres and efforts made to improve future stock of the breed. 69▶

Below: The impressive Bouvier des Flandres makes an effective guard.

BRIARD

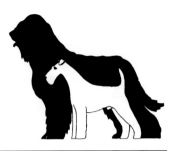

Good points
- *Easy to train*
- *Family pet and/or farm worker*
- *Gentle nature*
- *Good guard dog*
- *Weather-proof coat*
- *Successful show dog*
- *Loyal*

Take heed
- *No drawbacks known*

The Briard is the best-known of the four French sheepdogs—the others being the Beauceron, the Picardy and the Pyrenean Mountain Dog—although the latter won Best in Show at Crufts in 1970. Briards are good-natured, and can be kept happily either as an affectionate family pet, or for work around the farm; quite a number are finding their way into the show ring.

Size
Height: dog 58.5-68.5cm (23-27in); bitch 56-65cm (22-25½in).

Exercise
Regular, and not just a walk around the park.

Grooming
Regular brushing. The Briard takes pride in cleaning itself.

Feeding
Recommended would be 1½-2½ cans (376g, 13.3oz size) of a branded meaty product, with biscuit added in equal part by volume; or 5 cupfuls of a dry food, complete diet, mixed in the proportion of 1 cup of feed to ½ cup of hot or cold water.

Origin and history
The Briard comes from the Brie area of France, where it is also known as the Berger de Brie or Chien de Brie. It has been known since the 12th century. There is an entertaining 14th century French legend of how the Briard was given its name: in the year 1371 Sir Aubry de Montdidier was assassinated. His killer was hunted down by his dog, and it was ordained by the king that a battle should take place between the man, named Macaire, and the dog The battle took place on the Isle of Notre Dame, and the dog proved the victor. Macaire then admitted his crime and was beheaded. It is likely that from then on the Briard became known as the Chien d'Aubry, and a shield sculpted in stone was placed in the church at Montdidier, bearing a likeness of a dog's head that looks similar to the Briard of today. 69▶

Below: The Briard is an active and lively breed that can become a devoted pet and a trusted worker.

HUNGARIAN KUVASZ

Good points
- *Intelligent*
- *Excellent guard*
- *Loyal*
- *Tireless worker*
- *Gentle and patient*

Take heed
- *Tends to be a one-person dog*
- *Sensitive – should not be dealt with harshly*

The Hungarian Kuvasz may be kept as a pet and is loyal and devoted to its owner and family. It is. however, essentially a guard and will be ever watchful for intruders. It is an intelligent dog, and its name comes from a Turkish word meaning 'guardian of the peace'. It is a natural herder and has been used for big game hunting. It resembles the Slovakian Kuvasz which is a smaller breed.

Size
Height at withers: dog 71-75cm (28-29½in); bitch 66-70cm (26-27½). Weight: dog 39.9-52.2kg (88-115lb); bitch 30-42.2kg (66-93lb).

Exercise
Needs plenty of exercise.

Below: The Hungarian Kuvasz is devoted to its owners but will treat strangers with suspicion.

Grooming
Regular brushing will keep the coat in good condition.

Feeding
Recommended would be 1½-2½ cans of a branded meaty product (376g, 13.3oz size), with biscuit added in equal part by volume; or 5 cupfuls of a dry food, complete diet, mixed in the proportion of 1 cup of feed to ½ cup of hot or cold water.

Origin and history
The Kuvasz has existed in Hungary for centuries, and as early as the 1490s was protecting Hungarian nobility against possible assassins. It became known as the guard dog of the privileged, only the high-born being permitted to keep one. It is a breed that has to date attained greater popularity in the United States than in Great Britain, where there are very few. 70▶

BERNESE MOUNTAIN DOG (Bernese Sennenhund)

Good points
- *Beautiful*
- *Easily trained*
- *Excellent watchdog*
- *Good with other animals and people*
- *Suitable as a pet*

Take heed
- *No drawbacks known, but it is a big dog to have around the place*

The Bernese Mountain Dog is the most internationally known of the four Swiss Mountain Dogs, the others being the Great Swiss Sennenhund (or Mountain Dog), the Appenzell Sennenhund and the Entlebuch Sennenhund. It is used as both draught dog and companion in its country of origin, but elsewhere it is gaining popularity as pet and show dog, being easy to train despite its size and strength, loyal, affectionate and docile with both other animals and humans. It is a beautiful dog, with something of the Collie in its appearance.

Size
Dog 63.5-70cm (25-27½in); bitch 58.5-66cm (23-26in).

Exercise
Needs a reasonable amount of exercise and is not ideally suited to town life or apartment living.

Below: The loyal Bernese, used as a draught dog for centuries.

Grooming
Regular brushing will keep the coat in good condition.

Feeding
Recommended would be 1½-2½ cans (376g, 13.3oz size) of a branded meaty product, with biscuit added in equal part by volume; or 5 cupfuls of a dry food, complete diet, mixed in the proportion of 1 cup of feed to ½ cup of hot or cold water.

Origin and history
The Bernese has been used as both herder and draught dog for centuries, and many a visitor to Switzerland returns with a snapshot of a Sennenhund pulling a milk cart. The types of Sennenhund are named after the regions in which they were found. They have Mastiff characteristics and are believed to have Molossian ancestry. The St Bernard, Rottweiler and Newfoundland are also related to the Sennenhunds. 70▶

ESTRELA MOUNTAIN DOG (Cão Serra da Estrela)

Good points
- *Excellent guard dog*
- *Can live in harmony with other dogs*

Take heed
- *A reserved dog with strangers*
- *Will wander if not properly enclosed*
- *Needs firm, but affectionate handling*

The Estrela Mountain Dog is a hardy animal of great power. A really excellent guard dog, it was bred to guard the flocks in the Sierra da Estrela range against wolves and marauders, and has considerable stamina. Very loyal and affectionate to its owners, but rather indifferent to others, the Estrela is intelligent and alert, but inclined to be stubborn.

The Estrela needs a special kind of home with a great deal of love, but a firm hand.

Size
Dogs: 65-76cm (25½-30in).
Bitches: 62-72·5cm (24½-28½in).

Exercise
Needs plenty of exercise.

Grooming
Regular brushing will keep the coat in good condition. The worst of the moult is quickly dealt with.

Feeding
The Estrela prefers a light diet, green tripe being a favourite. Rich, red meat is not often welcome. Biscuit is occasionally accepted. In puppyhood milk feeds are rejected at an early stage, while adults will have self imposed periods of starvation with no ill effect. The diet is sometimes a problem as Estrelas prefer a mild diet and are unlike most other breeds in their eating habits.

Origin and history
This is a dog that has existed for centuries in the Estrela mountains of Portugal. It resembles the St.

Above: The Estrela Mountain Dog, a natural guard dog that needs firm, kind handling as a pet.

Bernard, but is of lighter stature with something of the Mastiff in its make-up. It was bred as a herder and guard dog.

The Estrela Mountain Dog was first introduced into the United Kingdom by Mr. Roger Pye, who sent a bitch whelp from Portugal in 1974. She produced seven pups, five dogs and two bitches, in the UK, the latter remaining while the mother returned to Portugal. Four of the pups were destined for Mrs. Marcia Dovey's Sturtmoor Kennel near Salisbury in Wiltshire. Sturtmoor has won five Top Estrela Awards. 71▶

ANATOLIAN SHEPHERD DOG

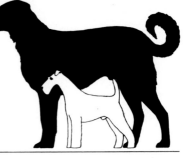

Good points
- *Affectionate*
- *Hardy and independent*
- *Intelligent*
- *Loyal*
- *Trainable*

Take heed
- *Not suited to town life*
- *Will accept others, but main loyalty remains with owner*

The Anatolian Shepherd Dog is a shepherd's guard dog of ancient lineage. It is a large, vigorous outdoor working dog with a self-sufficient temperament. Such dogs are found from the Anatolian plateau of Turkey right across Afghanistan. The shepherds of Central Asia crop their dogs' ears and give them massive iron-spiked collars to help the dog defend the flocks from predators.

The Anatolian Shepherd Dog can live outside, but it is much better to allow it in the house as part of the family, where it will become more amenable.

This is a dog that will automatically identify with one person as its owner. It will accept other members of the family, and friends who have been introduced, but its main loyalty will remain with its owner.

It needs and responds to a great deal of love, and should be taken around and socialized at an early age, otherwise it may become too possessive. The Anatolian Shepherd Dog's inclination is to be friendly with other animals and it has a very long memory. Incidentally, when it leans heavily against you, this means that you have been totally accepted.

Size
Weight: dog 49.9-64kg (110-141lb); bitch 41-59kg (90-130lb). Height: dog 73.5-8.1cm (29-32in) at the shoulder; bitch 71-78.5cm (28-31in) at the shoulder.

Exercise
The Anatolian Shepherd Dog is not suited to town life, because it needs plenty of space in which to work off its energy, This it will do on its own, so normally there is no need to walk it in the conventional way. Indeed, it is said that a man would have to walk all day to give such a dog enough movement for it to be able to develop its superb body. The breed is naturally active and playful and will be happy in a large and well-fenced garden.

For a big dog, the Anatolian Shepherd Dog moves remarkably quickly and gracefully, and speeds of 55kph (34mph) have been clocked up by the breed.

Grooming
The natural inclination of this breed is to get up at intervals, especially at night, and patrol the area, bedding down in a different spot each time. This keeps its coat remarkably clean, odourless and free of parasites. However, the coat will certainly benefit from regular, thorough brushing.

Feeding
The canned food requirement for a dog of this size is approximately 3 cans per day (376g, 13.3oz size), with biscuit supplement in equal part by volume, or the fresh meat equivalent, so they are by no means cheap to feed. Incidentally, all so-called soft bones may be given and are probably a necessity for the animal's proper development.

However, it is of interest that in their own country they can exist on very little, and shepherds have recounted with pride how their

ANATOLIAN SHEPHERD DOG

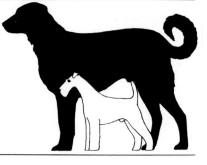

Above: The Anatolian Shepherd Dog has exceptional stamina and hardiness, developed over centuries as a shepherd dog.

dogs remained with the flocks for up to a week without food or water. They have two strange behavioural adaptations to help them survive, one being an alert 'hibernation' in the cruel midday Turkish sun, the other an ability to dig up gophers— a kind of prairie dog or marmot-like animal—for food.

Origin and history
Since Babylonian times, there existed in this area a breed of large, strong dogs with a heavy head. They were employed as war dogs, and for hunting big game such as lions and horses. Some spectacular examples can be seen on the very well preserved bas-reliefs in the Assyrian Room of the British Museum in London.

In their native Turkey the dogs do not herd the sheep, but patrol around them, often seeking higher ground to get a better view and a breeze. The dogs patrol the ground ahead of the flock, checking out every bush and irregularity of the terrain for potential trouble. Should they notice anything, even a moving car, they will, silently at first, split up and converge upon it at great speed. These ambush tactics are completely inborn and fascinating to watch. 71▶

TIBETAN MASTIFF

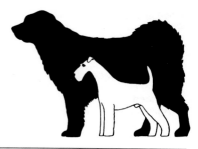

Good points
- *Handsome*
- *Strongly built*
- *Excellent guard dog*
- *Reliable temperament unless provoked*
- *Loyal to owner*

Take heed
- *Suspicious of strangers*

The Tibetan Mastiff bears a strong resemblance to the St Bernard. It is an excellent guard dog, but is good-natured unless provoked. It can be kept happily as a reliable companion/guard.

Size
Height at shoulder: dog 63.5-68.5cm (25-27in); bitch 56-61cm (22-24in).

Exercise
Needs regular vigorous exercise.

Grooming
Daily brushing will keep the coat in good, healthy condition.

Feeding
Recommended would be 1½-2½ cans (376g, 13.3oz size) of a branded meaty product, with biscuit added in equal part by volume; or 5 cupfuls of a dry food, complete diet, mixed in the proportion of 1 cup of feed to ½ cup of hot or cold water.

Origin and history
The Tibetan Mastiff is regarded as a British breed, but it originated in Central Asia. where its job was to guard flocks. Like other Mastiffs, it is likely to have descended from the Roman Molossus. 71▶

Below: The Tibetan Mastiff is a powerful guard dog from Central Asia. Basically a docile breed with strong allegiance to its owner, it will deter intruders with a show of force.

BORZOI

Good points
- *Aloof*
- *Beautiful and graceful*
- *Intelligent*
- *Faithful*
- *Striking show dog*

Take heed
- *A dignified dog, not ideal as a children's playmate*
- *Not suitable for apartments*

The Borzoi is an animal of great beauty and grace used in Russia from the 17th century for wolf hunting and coursing. Today it is often regarded more as a fashion accessory: the fur-clad silent film star accompanied by two Borzois was not a rarity!

They are dignified, good-natured animals, but somewhat aloof and not likely to enjoy playing wild games with children.

Size
Height at shoulder: dog from 73.5cm (29in) upwards; bitch from 68.5cm (27in) upwards.

Exercise
The Borzoi needs a great deal of exercise, but remember that this dog is a hunter: it is essential that it should be allowed to run only when far from livestock.

Feeding
Recommended would be 1½-2½ cans (376g, 13.3oz size) of a branded meaty product, with biscuit added in equal part by volume; or 5 cupfuls of a dry food, complete diet, mixed in the proportion of 1 cup of feed to ½ cup of hot or cold water.

Origin and history
The Borzoi was maintained for centuries by the Czars and noblemen of Imperial Russia for hunting the wolf. During the 15th and 16th centuries it was crossed with the sheepdog to provide strength, and later with various hounds to obtain more speed. However it was from the strain developed by the Grand Duke Nicolai Nicolayevitch that the present-day standard evolved. Information on present-day Borzois in the USSR is sketchy. There would appear to be more Borzois in fashionable capital cities of the world such as New York, London and Paris. 71▶

Below: Borzois combine elegance with great power and speed.

DEERHOUND (Scottish Deerhound)

Good points
- *Graceful and beautiful*
- *Hardy*
- *Happy to be with humans and to please*
- *Loving*
- *Sound temperament*

Take heed
- *No drawbacks known, if you have sufficient space*

The Deerhound is a creature of grace and beauty, mentioned frequently in the novels of Sir Walter Scott. It is strong and healthy, anxious to please and asks no more than to be its owner's devoted companion.

Size
Weight: dog 38.5-47.6kg (85-105lb); bitch 29.5-36.3kg (65-80lb). Height at shoulder: dog not less than 76cm (30in); bitch 71cm (28in).

Exercise
Needs a great deal of exercise.

Grooming
Requires very little trimming, just removal of extra shaggy hairs for show, and regular brushing. Its coat is weather-resistant, and this breed rarely feels the cold — in fact, it seems to prefer it.

Feeding
Recommended would be 1½-2½ cans (376g, 13.3oz size) of a branded meaty product, with biscuit added in equal part by volume; or 5 cupfuls of a dry food, complete diet, mixed in the proportion of 1 cup of feed to ½ cup of hot or cold water. Will need extra feed if used for coursing.

Origin and history
The Deerhound was purpose-bred to hunt with its master by day and to grace his sumptuous dining hall at night. With the advent of breech-loading rifles, the need for the hunting Deerhound ceased, as did its popularity; in Britain, it is

Above: Capable of great speed as a hunting dog, the Deerhound is now kept mainly as a companion, a role it fulfills superbly. As a pet the Deerhound is obedient, quiet and extremely faithful.

now kept only by devotees of the breed. It is said that once you have owned a Deerhound, never again do you wish to own another breed. It is truly a gentle giant.

The breed has much of the Greyhound in its make-up, and it seems that until the 19th century the Irish Wolfhound and the Deerhound were of a similar type. Today it is easy to distinguish between the two, the Deerhound being a sleeker, lighter dog. 72▶

IRISH WOLFHOUND

Good points
- *Quiet and friendly*
- *Marvellous with children*
- *Good guard*
- *Happiest as a housedog*
- *Magnificent show dog*

Take heed
- *Gentle when stroked, fierce when provoked*
- *Needs discipline as a puppy*

The Irish Wolfhound, variously known as the Wolfdog, the Irish Greyhound and the Great Dog of Ireland, is a gentle giant, fierce only when provoked. It is intelligent, intensely loyal and slow to anger. Irish Wolfhounds do, nonetheless, have a mind of their own, so firm, gentle discipline is advocated in puppyhood.

Size
The minimum height and weight of dogs should be 78.5cm (31in) and 54.4kg (120lb); of bitches 71cm (28in) and 40.8kg (90lb). Anything below this should be heavily penalized. Great size, including height at shoulder and proportionate length of body, is the target to be aimed for, and ideally the breed should average 81-86cm (32-34in) in dogs, showing the requisite power, activity, courage and symmetry.

Exercise
Despite its size, the Irish Wolfhound does not require more exercise than smaller breeds, but it should have ample space in which to gambol. Let it have unrestricted play during puppyhood, but do not force it to take lengthy walks, rather allowing it to 'muscle up' by its own joyful activity. Irish Wolfhounds are usually taught both to walk and to move at the trot while being led; as they are so powerful, obedience is essential.

Grooming
Brush regularly, and remove long, straggly hairs from ears, neck and underside with finger and thumb.

This is a natural-looking breed, which is not difficult to groom.

Feeding
At least 2½ cans (376g, 13.3oz size) of a branded meaty product, with biscuit added in equal part by volume; or 5 cupfuls of a dry food, complete diet, mixed in the proportion of 1 cup of feed to ½ cup of hot or cold water.

Origin and history
The Irish Wolfhound is the national dog of Ireland, and its original role was to kill wolves. It is spoken of in many legends, but almost certainly came from Greece with the invading Celts, circa 279 BC. The best-known story of an Irish Wolfhound concerns the dog Gelert, given as a gift to Llewellyn, Prince of Wales, by King John of England around 1210. Prince Llewellyn went hunting, leaving the faithful Gelert in charge of his baby son. On his return he could see only Gelert, with blood on its mouth, and, thinking it had killed the child, he drew his sword and slew the dog. It was only then that he saw, nearby, the body of a wolf, and heard the happy chuckle of his child. Gelert had killed the wolf and saved the child. Full of remorse, Prince Llewellyn ordered a statue to be erected in memory of Gelert, and the dog's name has lived on through the centuries.

The first breed standard for the Irish Wolfhound was set down in 1885, after Captain George Graham, a Scot in the British Army, had spent 23 years restoring the breed from near extinction. 72▶

LEONBERGER

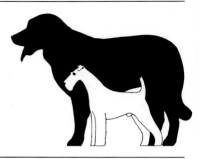

Good points
- *Derived from sound breeds*
- *Handsome*
- *Lively temperament*
- *Intelligent*
- *Good watchdog*

Take heed
- *Little known outside Germany, Holland, France and Belgium*
- *Needs plenty of space*

The Leonberger is a strong, sound dog, used for protecting livestock and as a draught dog in Western Germany and certain other European countries. It was derived from animals of sound temperament, and is beginning to create interest internationally. A breed member was exhibited at Crufts soon after World War II, but it is doubtful if any specimens were bred in England.

Size
Height: dog 76cm (30in); bitch 70cm (27½in).

Exercise
Would need adequate space and exercise to thrive.

Grooming
Normal daily brushing needed.

Feeding
Recommended would be 1½-2½ cans (376g, 13.3oz size) of a branded meaty product, with biscuit added in equal part by volume; or 5 cupfuls of a dry food, complete diet, mixed in the proportion of 1 cup of feed to ½ cup of hot or cold water.

Origin and history
The Leonberger is a German dog derived through crossing the Landseer-type Newfoundland with the Pyrenean Mountain Dog, the result being a most attractive breed of yellow to reddish brown colour that is gradually becoming known outside Germany and the bordering countries. 73▶

Below: The strong and elegant Leonberger, an attractive watchdog.

PYRENEAN MOUNTAIN DOG (Great Pyrenees)

Good points
- *Can be kept indoors or outdoors*
- *Easy to train*
- *Family protector*

Take heed
- *A working dog, happiest with a job to do*
- *Does not like strangers taking liberties*
- *Needs plenty of space*

The Pyrenean Mountain Dog is a natural shepherd dog bred to guard flocks in the Pyrenees. Nonetheless it has become a popular household pet with those who have the space and income to keep such a large dog. Mr and Mrs Prince's Bergerie Knur won Best in Show at Crufts in 1970.

They are hardy and good-natured, and become devoted to the entire family. They are not keen on approaches from strangers, however, and accidents have occurred when show visitors have been tempted to give a pat.

Size
Height at shoulder: dog at least 71cm (28in); bitch at least 66cm (26in). Weight: dog at least 49.9kg (110lb); bitch at least 40.8kg (90lb).

Exercise
Normal requirements. Strangely, for such a big fellow, the Pyrenean will adapt to town or country, and be content with walks of average length. Its gait is unhurried, giving the impression of a powerful animal moving steadily and smoothly.

Grooming
Regular brushing will keep the coat in good condition.

Feeding
Recommended: at least 2½ cans (376g, 13.3oz size) of a branded meaty product, with biscuit added in equal part by volume; or 5 cupfuls of a dry food, complete diet, mixed in the proportion of 1 cup of feed to ½ cup of hot or cold water.

Above: The Pyrenean Mountain Dog, one of the largest and strongest of present-day breeds. Given plenty of space, it will make a trustworthy and easy-going companion.

Origin and history
The Pyrenean was a royal favourite in the French court before the revolution. It has never regained the same popularity, though it is widely known and frequently exhibited. It comes from the area from which it takes its name and was once used to guard sheep, and also fortresses, wearing a spiked collar like that of the Mastiff. The breed became known when shepherds found a ready market for their pups with tourists.

73▶

MAREMMA SHEEPDOG (Pastore Maremmano Abruzzese)

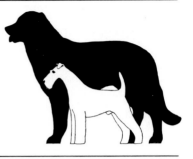

Good points
- *Great stamina*
- *Beautiful*
- *Intelligent*
- *Natural guarding instinct*
- *Weather-proof coat*

Take heed
- *Will treat its master as an equal – this breed is not renowned for obedience*

The Maremma is a dog that cannot tolerate discipline and, although it becomes fond of its master, it would consider it a weakness to show it. The dog will guard the entrance to its master's home, but will not lie across his feet. It will not forget kindness, or forgive injury, and will protect the family. The task of this breed was never to work sheep as would a Collie or German Shepherd Dog, but to defend the flocks from wolves, bears and thieves.

Size
Some latitude permitted with a minimum of 65cm (25½in) for a dog, 60cm (23½in) for a bitch.

Exercise
Exercise is a necessity for the breed's well-being in its formative years, but excessive exercise is not a vital need when the animal is mature. Rather than covering a long distance, their daily walks should be made as varied and interesting as possible, and – despite the fact that they are not particularly obedient – it is important that they should have some off-the-lead freedom. Walking on a hard surface will help to keep the dog's nails in condition. Rain will not have an adverse effect on the Maremma's coat. All it needs after a soaking is a good rub down. The dog will clean itself and soon be gleaming white again!

Grooming
Grooming should be carried out regularly, preferably with a wire dog brush and the occasional use of a good cleansing powder. A bath should be given once a year – more often if absolutely necessary – but this is a scrupulously clean breed that attends to its toilet fastidiously. During grooming the ears should be checked carefully for infection.

Feeding
The diet of the Maremma must contain adequate calcium, which can be given in either tablet or powder form. It is very necessary because of the extraordinary growth rate of Maremma puppies. Two meals daily are recommended for the breed, with perhaps some 'goodnight' biscuits. Recommended would be 1½-2½ cans of a branded canned product (376g, 13.3oz size), with biscuit added in equal parts by volume; or 5 cupfuls of a dry food, complete diet, mixed in the proportion of 1 cup of feed to ½ cup of hot or cold water.

Origin and history
It is believed that the Maremma sheepdog may have evolved from the ancient white working dog of the Magyars, and they have been bred exceedingly true to type on the Maremma plains and hills by Tuscan farmers.

The first known record of what is believed to be the Maremma was made 2000 years ago when Columbella (about AD 65) mentioned a white dog, and Marcus Varro (116-27 BC) gives a standard for a sheepdog that would seem to describe the Maremma of today. 73▶

KOMONDOR

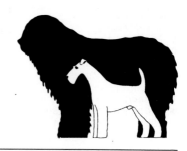

The Komondor (pronounced Koh-mohn-dohr—the plural is Komondorok) is a large white dog of imposing bearing, very strong and agile for its size. Nobody can mistake a grown dog for any other breed. It is covered with a full coat falling in tassels or cords and looks like an old-fashioned string mop.

This is a loyal dog whose purpose in life is to guard the property and charges in its care. It does not attack without provocation but trespassers will not be tolerated.

Size
Weight: dog about 49.9-61.2kg (110-135lbs); bitch about 36.3-49.9kg (80-110lb). Height: dog average 80cm (31½in), minimum 66cm (26in); bitch average 70cm (27½in), minimum 60cm (23½in).

Exercise
Puppies are large and active and require a lot of exercise for good development. A grown dog is maintained in good condition on a moderate amount of exercise. In a city this will have to be given on a lead.

Grooming
The Komondor has a thick, heavy, double coat; the shorter undercoat is woolly and soft, the outer coat longer, coarse and wavy. The combination of the two types of hair forms naturally into tassel-like cords, the cords being a type of controlled matting.It is never brushed or combed. It forms naturally, with the owner aiding by controlling the size of the cords in areas where matting is too large.

Bath the Komondor when it gets dirty, wetting the coat thoroughly and using a canine shampoo; rinse thoroughly, and wring with towels. A grown dog will take a long time to dry. Cords do not come out when you wash the dog; indeed, they will tighten up with age and washing. The dog requires standard care for eyes, pads and nails.

Feeding
Recommended: at least 2½ cans of a branded canned product (376g, 13.3oz size), with biscuit added in equal parts by volume; or 5 cupfuls of a dry food, complete diet, mixed in the proportion of 1 cup of feed to ½ cup of hot or cold water.

Origin and history
The Komondor was bred for centuries to guard flocks and property from thieves and predators on the Hungarian plains. It has worked with and without other dogs, first herding the semi-wild Hungarian sheep, later protecting whatever herds and property required a large and commanding dog as guard. Bred into the dog is an instinct to guard and to take responsibility for making decisions. The Komondor naturally protects whatever is entrusted to it—if not sheep, then goats, cattle, and chickens on a farm or ranch, or cats, dogs and children if it is a family companion. 73▶

BULLMASTIFF

Good points
- *Affectionate*
- *Trustworthy*
- *First-class guard*
- *Good with children*

Take heed
- *Remember its ferocious past;
  if you have one, make sure it is
  trained and temperamentally
  sound*

The Bullmastiff is an extremely strong breed, obtained through crossing the Mastiff with the Bulldog. At one time it had an almost unequalled reputation for ferocity, but today's specimens tend to be lovable and trustworthy, despite their power and size.

Size
Height at shoulder: dog 63.5-68.5cm (25-27in); bitch 61-66cm (24-26in). Weight: dog 49.9-59kg (110-130lb); bitch 40.8-49.9kg (90-110lb).

Exercise
Needs regular exercise. A child or lightweight adult would not be able to hold on to the lead.

Grooming
Regular brushing will keep the coat in good condition.

Feeding
Recommended: at least 2½ cans (376g, 13.3oz size) of a branded meaty product, with biscuit added in equal part by volume; or 5 cupfuls of a dry food, complete diet, mixed in the proportion of 1 cup of feed to ½ cup of hot or cold water.

Origin and history
The Bullmastiff is said to have been evolved 200 or 300 years ago by crossing the Mastiff with the Bulldog, as a guard dog against poachers, the bulk of the dog weighing down intruders without actually harming them. It was not until later that they attained their reputation for ferocity, despite novelist Charlotte Brontë's loving references to her Bullmastiff Tartar. Nowadays the breed has become a big softie whose appearance alone would deter. However, such large dogs need skilful handling. 74▶

Below: The Bullmastiff looks fierce but will make a lovable pet with sensible handling and training.

NEAPOLITAN MASTIFF

The Neapolitan Mastiff is a large, imposing dog, usually depicted wearing a spiked collar. It is an excellent guard, but is reputed to have a docile and friendly temperament, being unlikely to attack except on command.

Size
Height: dog 65-72.5cm (25½-28½in), bitch 60-68.5cm (23½-27in). Weight: 49.9-68kg (110-150lb).

Exercise
Like most dogs of its size, it is happiest when given a job to do and with a reasonable area in which to exercise.

Grooming
Regular brushing will keep the coat in good condition.

Feeding
Recommended: at least 2½ cans (376g, 13.3oz size) of a branded meaty product, with biscuit added in equal part by volume; or 5 cupfuls of a dry food, complete diet, mixed as 1 cup of feed to ½ cup of water.

Origin and history
One scientific classification of the Neapolitan Mastiff puts it in the Molossoid group. It is a guard and defence dog, a police dog and a tracker, of Italian origin, more specifically Neapolitan. Whether Italy's Mastiff ever did battle in the arenas of Rome is debatable, but geographical evidence gives credence to this theory. 74▶

Below: The forbidding Neapolitan Mastiff, rarely seen outside Italy.

MASTIFF

Good points
- *Brave*
- *Good-natured*
- *Excellent guard*
- *Intelligent*
- *Loyal*
- *Quietly dignified*

Take heed
- *Likes to have a job to do*

The Mastiff is a large, powerful dog that makes a formidable guard and loyal companion, becoming devoted to its owners. It is suspicious of strangers, and happiest when given a job to do.

Size
Height at shoulder: dog 76cm (30in), bitch 70cm (27½in).

Exercise
Regular normal exercise, but preferably with a purpose.

Grooming
Daily brushing will keep the coat in good condition.

Feeding
Recommended: at least 2½ cans (376g, 13.3oz size) of a branded meaty product, with biscuit added in equal part by volume; or 5 cupfuls of a dry food, complete diet, mixed in the proportion of 1 cup of feed to ½ cup of hot or cold water.

Health care
Their size can contribute to limb joint problems. Check with your veterinarian if you suspect trouble.

Origin and history
The Mastiff is an ancient breed that was treasured by the Babylonians, fought in the arenas of Rome, and has lived in Britain since the time of Julius Caesar. In the Middle Ages the Mastiff was used as a guard dog and also for hunting. St Bernard blood has been introduced, in an effort to restore the Mastiff to something of the size of its early splendour Numbers today are fairly low. 74▶

Below: One of the world's well-established breeds, the Mastiff commands respect by virtue of its sheer size and noble bearing.

GIANT SCHNAUZER

Good points
- *Easy to train*
- *Excellent with children*
- *Fearless*
- *Fine guard*
- *Good-natured*
- *Playful*

Take heed
- *Slow to mature*
- *Wary of strangers*

The Giant Schnauzer is the largest of the three Schnauzer varieties, (the other being Miniature and Standard), with which it shares the qualities of good humour, intelligence and devotion. It has been used for security and as a messenger in the armed services; it works well in obedience competitions, and is a good ratter — ratting was, after all, the Schnauzer's original job. However, this giant variety is little seen in America or Great Britain, where the Miniature variety is popular, but the Standard Schnauzer less so.

Size
Height: dog 65-70cm (25½-27½in); bitch 60-65cm (23½-25½in).

Exercise
Needs plenty of vigorous exercise.

Grooming
This is a breed that requires a certain amount of care if it is to do its owner justice. Daily grooming with a wire brush or glove is necessary, and those quizzical whiskers have to be combed. The coat has to be stripped with a serrated stripping comb, or the dead hair plucked out with finger and thumb. Ask the breeder for a grooming chart, or at least a demonstration, before tackling the job yourself — especially if your heart is set on the show ring.

Feeding
Recommended: at least 2½ cans (376g, 13.3oz size) of a branded meaty product, with biscuit added in equal part by

Above: The Giant Schnauzer, a lively, good humoured companion.

volume; or 5 cupfuls of a dry food, complete diet, mixed in the proportion of 1 cup of feed to ½ cup of hot or cold water.

Origin and history
Descended from German sheepdogs and cattle dogs, this, the largest Schnauzer, was evolved through interbreeding with the smaller Schnauzer varieties. It was first shown in Munich in October 1909 under the name 'Russian bear Schnauzer', the breed being classified as a working dog in Germany in 1925. 74▶

GREAT DANE

Good points
- *Devoted*
- *Gets on with other animals*
- *Good-natured*
- *Easy to train*

Take heed
- *Not the dog to have a rough and tumble with — it might take it seriously!*
- *Not renowned for longevity*

The Great Dane is a wonderful companion, devoted to the family, slow to anger and ready to accept other pets. Despite its size it does not object to apartment life, provided it has plenty of walks. It is easily trained. Regrettably this is a breed that is not renowned for its longevity.

Size
Minimum height: dog 76cm (30in); bitch 71cm (28in). Weight: dog 54.4kg (120lb); bitch 45.4kg (100lb).

Exercise
Regular exercise on hard ground would be recommended.

Grooming
Daily grooming with a body brush. *NB* The Great Dane needs warm sleeping quarters.

Feeding
Recommended would be up to 4 cans (376g, 13.3oz size) of a branded meaty product, with biscuit added in equal part by volume; or 5 cupfuls of a dry food, complete diet, mixed in the proportion of 1 cup of feed to ½ cup of hot or cold water.

Origin and history
The Great Dane has existed in Britain for many centuries and is thought to be a descendant of the Molossus hounds of Roman times. In the Middle Ages they were used to chase wild boar, to bait bulls and as body guards.

Interest in the breed was roused in Germany in the 1800s by

Above: The Great Dane is a truly magnificent breed in temperament, size, stamina and devotion.

Bismarck, who had a penchant for the Mastiff, and by crossing the Mastiff of southern Germany and the Great Dane of the north produced a Dane similar to the type known today. It was first exhibited at Hamburg in 1863, being shown under the separate varieties of Ulmer Dogge and Dänisch Dogge. In 1876, it was decided that they should be shown under the single heading of Deutsche Dogge, and they were acclaimed as the national dog of Germany. This breed is sometimes referred to as the Apollo of the dog world. 74▶

ST BERNARD

Good points
- *Friendly*
- *Loyal*
- *Adores children*
- *Easy to train*
- *Supremely intelligent*

Take heed
- *Hindquarters prone to weakness*
- *Needs plenty of space*
- *Not renowned for longevity*

The St Bernard is a gentleman; powerful, but gentle. It adores children and is loyal and affectionate, coupled with which it is supremely intelligent and proves very easy to train.

Size
The taller the better, provided that symmetry is maintained; thoroughly well proportioned, and of great substance.

Exercise
Do not give the young St Bernard too much exercise. Short, regular walks are advocated, rather than long, tiring ones.

Grooming
Daily brushing will be sufficient.

Feeding
Frecommended would be up to 4 cans (376g, 13.3oz size) of a branded meaty product, with biscuit added in equal part by volume; or 5 cupfuls of a dry food, complete diet, mixed in the proportion of 1 cup of feed to ½ cup of hot or cold water.

Origin and history
The St Bernard is a descendant of the Roman Molossian dogs. It is named after the St Bernard Hospice in the Swiss Alps, to which it was introduced between 1660 and 1670, where it became famed for rescuing climbers in the Alps. One dog, Barry, is credited with saving 40 lives between 1800 and 1810. The first St Bernard to come to Britain arrived in 1865. The breed had a boost in popularity in the 1950s, when a St Bernard played a prominent role in the British film *Genevieve*, and it is also associated by almost everyone with advertisements for a well-known brandy. 74▶

Below: The St Bernard is a powerful but benevolent giant of a breed.

NEWFOUNDLAND

Good points
- *Excellent guard, but fierce only when provoked*
- *Fine swimmer*
- *Marvellous with other animals and children*
- *Intelligent*
- *Affectionate*

Take heed
- *No drawbacks known*

The Newfoundland is a gentle protector of children and family that gets on well with other animals and makes a thoroughly reliable companion and guard; it is slow to attack unless provoked.

Size
Average height at shoulders: dog 71cm (28in); bitch 66cm (26in). Weight: dog 63.5-68kg (140-150lb); bitch 49.9-54.4kg (110-120lb).

Exercise
Regular exercise on hard ground.

Grooming
Daily brushing with a hard brush.

Feeding
Recommended would be up to 4 cans (376g, 13.3oz size) of a branded meaty product, with biscuit added in equal part by volume; or 5 cupfuls of a dry food, complete diet, mixed in the proportion of 1 cup of feed to ½ cup of hot or cold water.

Origin and history
The Newfoundland is the traditional life-saving dog, an animal with the over-powering instinct to carry anything in the water safely ashore. It originates from the north-east of Canada, into whose protective harbours fishing boats of other nations have habitually come to avoid bad weather. It is believed that ships' dogs mated with the local working dogs, whose ancestors probably included Red Indian dogs and Basque sheepdogs, to produce the Newfoundland. Particularly famous is the Landseer variety, with black and white markings; it is so named because of its portrayal by the British painter Sir Edward Landseer (1802-73). 74▶

Below: The Newfoundland is a gentle children's companion.

Index

Page numbers in Roman type refer to text entries; *italic* numbers refer to photographs; **bold** numbers to colour artwork illustrations.